Remember
the
Truth

真善忍

Remember the Truth

Believing in Goodness in Today's China

Hongwei Lou

with Kathryn Lovett

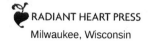
RADIANT HEART PRESS
Milwaukee, Wisconsin

Published by Radiant Heart Press,
an imprint of HenschelHAUS Publishing, Inc.
2625 S. Greeley St. Suite 201,
Milwaukee, Wisconsin, 53207
www.henschelHAUSbooks.com

ISBN: 978-1-59598-251-3
E-ISBN: 978-1-59598-258-2

Publisher's Cataloging-In-Publication Data
(Prepared by The Donohue Group, Inc.)
Lou, Hongwei.
Remember the truth : believing in goodness in today's China / Hongwei
Lou, with Kathryn Lovett.
p. : ill. ; cm.
Includes bibliographical references.
Issued also as an ebook.
ISBN: 978-1-59598-251-3
1. Lou, Hongwei. 2. Falun Gong (Organization) 3. Persecution—
China. 4. Freedom of religion—China. 5. Autobiography. I. Lovett,
Kathryn. II. Title.
BP605.F36 L68 2013   299/.51/092   2013944721

*A portion of the proceeds from the sale of this book
will be donated to Friends of Falun Gong, a nonprofit that supports
freedom of belief for those who practice Falun Gong.*

Printed in the United States of America.

Truthfulness
Compassion
Tolerance

CHAPTER ONE

My father was born in the late 1940s in Heilongjiang Province, in the Northeastern part of China, followed by seven brothers and sisters. My grandfather supported them all on his meager income as an elementary school teacher, while my grandmother stayed home to take care of the children.

Being the eldest, my father helped look after his younger siblings. He remembers at age 6 carrying a brother or sister on his back while helping his mother with the cooking. There was never enough food, and my father remembers trying to eat slowly so his brothers and sisters could have more.

Hunger was a major concern throughout my father's childhood and teenage years. Early in his life he began to dream of one day getting a good job and sending money home.

The day my father was to take the university entrance exams, his mother added a bit more rice to the family's porridge for breakfast to make it thicker, so my father wouldn't feel hungry halfway through the test. During that time in communist China, milk and eggs were nearly impossible to come by.

After the exam, my father was completely exhausted. He dug into his pocket for the five *fen* his mother had given him, then he walked to a nearby store and bought three sugar candies with the coins. After eating them, he rested for a while until he had the energy to walk home.

My father's teenage growth years occurred during the Great Famine of 1958–1961, the so-called "Great Leap Forward." Even as an adult, he ended up not much taller than his mother. But his strong will to change the situation of his family motivated him to study hard.

He was admitted to a university in Harbin City to study Mechanical Manufacturing. He chose that profession because at the time, the communist regime had led people to believe that the working class was the most honorable one. Since the reform and opening up in the 1980s, these workers have become the poorest class.

Upon graduation, my father was sent to a factory in Xinxiang City, Henan Province, where he worked as a technician. The city was 2,000 kilometers from his hometown, but he was given no choice in where he was assigned.

My mother is from Qingdao city in Shandong Province. When she was nine, both her parents died because they had no money to see a doctor. My mother's sister once told her a story. When my grandmother was young, she came down with a disease that caused swelling in the abdomen. At that time, Qingdao was under German rule. When they brought my grandmother to the hospital, the German "invaders" performed the surgery for her free of charge. My mother later wondered why it was that in the "New China," after the so-called "liberation," her mother was allowed to die because she didn't have enough money for medical treatment.

Having lost her parents at a young age, my mother was taken to live with her older brother in Beijing. Conditions were also poor at her brother's house, and her sister-in-law treated her badly. She resented my mother's presence because her own four children didn't have enough to eat as it was. She would often scold my mother for causing her nieces and nephews to go hungry.

My mother became timid and didn't dare to speak, feeling she was a huge burden. In order to become financially independent as soon as possible, she studied hard and was admitted to an aeronautics college in Beijing, also studying Mechanical Manufacturing.

Upon graduation, she was dispatched to the aircraft factory where my father was working, which is where they met. They didn't have any romantic stories to tell me, though. At that time, young people didn't really have an opportunity to socialize and meet people other than at work, so most marriages occurred between colleagues.

When my father began working, his seven brothers and sisters were still in school. Every month, he sent two thirds of his income home to his parents. He knew they would still need this money even if he were to get married, and he worried he wouldn't be able to find a girl who would agree to such an arrangement.

When he met my mother, he could see that she was an honest and kind soul, and he thought maybe she would understand his situation. There was an older woman also working there who enjoyed making matches between young people. My father asked her to talk with my mother and tell her that he wanted to see her.

Ever since my mother lost her parents, she had felt that no one cared about her. She was very touched when the matchmaker told her that my father liked her. She also understood that it was his duty to care for his siblings. After all, her own brother had raised her, even when he could not really afford it. She knew how hard it was for my father to send so much money home, but she felt it was the right thing for him to do, and that she would not resent it. Soon they were married.

———◆———

In August of 1969, a little more than a year after they were married, their first child was born in a small city by the Yellow River.

I arrived right in the midst of the Cultural Revolution in China. With money so tight, my mother could not quit her job to take care of me. She returned to work eight weeks after the delivery.

Both my parents came from other provinces, so any family members who might have been able to help with the baby all lived too far away. Every day, my mother would lock me in the house before she went to work. Around lunch time, she would hurry home to feed me. Due to her own poor nutrition, she didn't have enough milk, so she fed me egg and sugar water. At that time in China, a farmer who raised chickens would be chastised for "chasing the tail of capitalism," so eggs were an extreme rarity. Once a week, my father would bicycle to a farmer's house in the country to buy some cheap eggs. This was the only source of good nourishment for my mother and me.

On the day of my third birthday, my baby brother, Xiaoyu, was born. Our shared birthday, the seventh day of the seventh month of the Chinese Lunar Calendar, is the Chinese version of Valentine's Day.

As the lovers' fable goes, the beautiful Zhinv, seventh daughter of the Goddess, decided that heaven was a bit too dull for her liking, so she escaped to Earth. There she fell in love with a cowherd, Niulang, and they were quickly married. They were wonderfully happy together until her mother found out that Zhinv was married to a mere mortal. The Goddess rudely dragged her daughter back to heaven, and forced her to return to her boring job of weaving colors into the clouds.

Niulang was grieved at his wife's sudden disappearance. Seeing this, his loyal ox found a way to allow Niulang and his two children to get to heaven to look for Zhinv. When he arrived in heaven, the Goddess discovered him and became furious. She scratched a river in the sky with her hairpin so he could not cross.

The stars Altair and Vega, the two lovers, must stay on each side of the Milky Way, where they can only see each other across the wide river. However, once a year, all the magpies in the world take pity on them and fly to heaven to form a bridge so that the lovers may join together for a single night each year—the seventh night of the seventh moon.

After my brother's birth, my mother's health began to deteriorate. Several years before, when she had finished college at age 20, she had been forced to participate in a "Long March" that was supposed to mimic the Red Army's 1935 Long March, which had lasted over a year. The idea was ostensibly to inspire patriotism toward the Communist Party.

My mother had to carry bags weighing dozens of kilograms across mountains and rivers, sleeping in moist soil drenched by the rain. This ordeal lasted a month or two, leaving her with rheumatism. Thereafter, whenever it rained, all her joints would ache.

Now, besides having an introverted personality, she was often in pain, which upset her mood. After my brother was born, she simply did not have the energy to take care of both me and the baby.

When my brother turned one year old, my parents decided they had no choice but to take him to my father's hometown in Heilongjiang Province, 2,000 kilometers away, and let my grandparents look after him. This separation and future separations would later make me think of Zhinv and Niulang.

At the time, food was given out in rations. If you didn't have a register or ration book, you couldn't buy rice even if you had the money. So when my father made the trip back to Heilongjiang with my brother, he also carried several bags of rice that he and my mother had saved up, to ease the burden on my grandparents.

It took two days to travel from Henan to Heilongjiang by train, with a transfer in Beijing. I have no idea how my father was able to carry both my brother and more than 100 pounds of rice. When I asked him about it, he said it had been difficult, but was really nothing compared to the reason for the journey.

On the day my father was to leave his parents' house and leave my brother behind, 1-year-old Xiaoyu suddenly realized his father was planning to leave him there. He cried and cried, begging for his parents. My father was really torn and wanted to bring him back, but he couldn't forget the pain and hardships back home. With tears in his eyes, he left his son in Heilongjiang.

Even though my family lived in hardship, I don't remember feeling it much when I was very young. My parents were always thrifty, and they did whatever they needed to keep me fed, because they both knew the pain of hunger.

My mother had grown up beside the ocean and knew that fish were good for health. Whenever they had a little bit of cash, they would buy a fish for me. I thought eggs and fish were the best foods there were. Whenever I ate a fish, they would just sit there and watch me eat.

When my brother turned three, my father was able to bring him back home. I remember the day he came back—our mother bought a huge fish to celebrate.

Although I felt I had enough to eat growing up, I don't remember getting much of an education.

With 5,000 years of Chinese history, there were an infinite number of stories my parents could have told us. But since they raised us during the Cultural Revolution, they didn't have the time or energy to tell us stories. Most of the education I received from my loving parents was on how to keep myself safe during the chaos period.

Often what I was taught at my elementary school could only be called absurd. I could recite the entire textbook, but I didn't understand what it meant. The reason I memorized it was that I wanted to get a good grade on my tests. Almost all the test questions were fixed-answer, such as multiple choice, fill-in, or true-false. If you could memorize all the sentences in the textbook, you could get 100 percent on the tests. There were no open or essay questions because that would encourage creative thought.

The goal of the Chinese Communist Party (CCP) at that point was not to educate us, but to brainwash us—to provide us with the thoughts they wanted us to have, starting early in childhood. To that end, most of the test answers were written to praise the CCP.

I remember a formal essay in my textbook describing how Liu Shaoqi, the head of state from 1959 to 1968, was a bourgeois, a traitor, a capitalist, and a thief. I thought it was really funny and asked my teacher, "If he was so bad, why did Chairman Mao make him head of state?" The teacher panicked. "Hush! Don't ever say that again!"

In another formal article in our textbook, Confucius was described as a gangster and a rogue. Now the communist regime has set up some "Confucius Institutes" in Western countries, hoping to confuse foreigners into thinking the CCP still cares about China's ancient culture.

Our high school had no band or orchestra, but there was an arts and music class once a week. It was, however, just another form of CCP propaganda. I still remember the lyrics of one song: "Party, Party, you are my mother, it is your milk that nourishes me . . ."

Actually, nearly everything was like this. The songs, the art, all of it espoused the wonders of the CCP. As children, we took all this to be normal.

———•———

When I was in middle school, China began its opening up and economic reform. People were finally able to obtain a measure of economic freedom. We could now buy and sell and earn a bit of money for ourselves. Many people developed a clear goal: earn more money and improve the quality of their lives. Students also had a clear goal: study hard and find a good job.

At that point, I realized my parents had not been living a good life. It was not simply that we were so poor, it was also that, by necessity, their goal in life was to fight for survival. They had no spiritual goals at all.

I once asked them, "What is your biggest dream in life?"

Without any hesitation, my father said, "Our biggest dream is to make sure you have a blissful life." My mother agreed.

But what was a blissful life, anyway? I had no idea. Nevertheless, I made a goal for myself: I would help my parents lead a good life as soon as possible. That was the motivation that kept me going.

From as early as I can remember, my family lived in a tiny apartment of less than 50 square meters (about 500 square feet). Whenever my parents heard that their company was distributing new apartments, they would become quite anxious.

The company supervisor would first distribute apartments to his relatives. Then he gave them to the employees who would make the most trouble for him if they didn't get one. To save himself the effort of dealing with these people, he always gave any benefits to them. Honest people like my parents weren't going to make a fuss, so they were never in line for an apartment.

Ever since I was a young girl, my mother would often lament, "Honest people are always at a disadvantage!"

I would ask, "Then should I still be an honest person when I grow up?"

My mother would get a pained look on her face, then she would sigh and say, "Yes, you still have to be an honest person."

I decided that someday I would buy a big house for my parents, so that honest people could live a comfortable life, too.

In China in those times, all resources were controlled by the CCP. They allocated everything for us—food, clothing, housing, medicine, employment. They controlled everything in our lives. Of course, people were too afraid to demand justice. Instead, they'd usually fight among each other, trying to get what they needed by taking it from the people around them.

As for me, I've always sought a sort of peace and harmony in my mind, but the reality would usually end up forcing me to fight for things. This caused more than a little impetuousness and confusion in my young heart.

I never heard my parents complain about the CCP. I knew they feared it, though, because they often said to me and my brother, "You must never say anything bad about the Party—especially in public!"

After the reforms, it became possible for an ordinary family to have a better life. The way to achieve that was for the children to attend a university and get a good job. To attend a university, a student had to pass the national university entrance exams, given on July 7, 8, and 9 of each year.

There are many high school graduates, but only so many spots for college. It was like trying to squeeze a million-strong army single file across a narrow bridge. Three days of examinations could easily determine one's whole life. As a result, examination month earned the nickname *heise qi yue*, or "Black July."

I did quite well in middle school and earned a placement in the best high school in our town. My life in high school was simple. Besides schoolwork, I did chores at home. My only goal in life was to get into a university.

I did have some good friends in school, but we seldom went out after school. One reason was that we had so much homework we rarely finished before midnight. Another reason was that there wasn't much entertainment available. The only entertainment I remember was watching a movie once with some friends. Being with my friends was nice, but looking back, the movie was awful. The purpose of the movie was to remind us that our current happy life was provided by the Communist Party. After all, without the CCP, we might have starved to death. We knew nothing about other countries, where living conditions were far better.

From the first day of high school, our teachers started ranting about the college entrance exams. The ranting continued throughout the three years of high school, and we felt enormous pressure. In every senior classroom, there was a countdown plate displaying the number of days until the entrance exams. It felt hard to even breathe. When I was 16, I knew a senior who succumbed to depression and gave up.

A good friend living near me told me they didn't even have classes during senior year. "Every day, we do exam practice after exam practice, and nothing else."

At that time, my results were already among the top in the class. I decided I didn't want to do questions for a whole year to prepare for a three-day exam, so I chose to sit for the entrance exams at the end of my second year, in July 1986.

My goal was Peking University, the best university in China. However, my results weren't as good as I had hoped. If I went to Peking, I might not be able to study the program I wanted. In the end, I decided on Wuhan University's business school to study business administration. Actually, I didn't know anything about business administration. My only thought was that after I studied business, I could become a manager, earn money, and buy my parents a big house.

CHAPTER TWO

I arrived at Wuhan University in 1986. I felt a bit uneasy because I had never been on my own before.

It was a helpful tradition in many universities that returning students would help the newcomers for a couple of months. They gave information and advice, invited the freshmen to parties, and welcomed them into existing social circles.

One evening in late December, I found myself at a party where a group of students were chatting. I noticed one young man immediately. He had big, gentle eyes, and the expression in them seemed very familiar. He felt like someone in my family, like an old friend that I had known for many years. His name was Dongwei. Just watching him eased my homesickness.

I learned that he was a year ahead of me at the university. I didn't talk to him much. At that time, because of the influence of traditional Chinese culture, young men and women were still shy with each other. Even though I liked him, it wouldn't be proper to just strike up a conversation.

Because of this, fate had to work a little harder to get couples together. It did its job, and we kept running into each other by chance. I could feel our eyes start to glow when we conversed, and I felt a sense of happiness in my heart.

Sometimes certain students, including me and Dongwei, would get together after class and talk about life. We were all fascinated by philosophical questions such as: "In this boundless universe, how was human life created?" "Where do people go after death?" and "What is the real meaning of life?" No matter how deeply we probed, we never arrived at any answers.

After several months, there were some subtle changes. I wanted to see Dongwei more, and I paid special attention to his actions and words. I often spent a long time thinking about the things he said, and guessing at what the expression in his eyes might have meant.

At the same time, I realized another girl also liked Dongwei. This girl was passionate and ardent and lovable, and she told me about her secret love.

Before this, I didn't realize that liking someone could bring such heartache. I was anguished over what to do. On the one hand, I told myself that Dongwei and I were just friends, and this girl was a really nice girl. If she were a better match for him, then maybe I should hide my feelings and let her be with him.

On the other hand, I could see in Dongwei's eyes that he liked me. What if he really did prefer me? In that case, how could I pretend I didn't care? That wouldn't be right.

As it happened, for the next several weeks we were in a group most of the time, so there was no chance to ask him about his feelings. I waited with a heavy heart.

Finally, one day we ran into each other on campus and started walking together. We walked in the direction of my dorm, and while we walked, I thought about how I might approach the subject. As we got closer to my dorm, I knew I'd better hurry and say something, or he would leave and I'd continue to be in agony.

As casually as I could, I said, "So . . . do you have a girl in your heart?"

We stopped walking, and he stood gazing at me.

He didn't say anything, so I pressed, "Don't you want to tell me?"

He replied, "I have a girl in my eyes."

———— ◆ ————

Summer came quickly. We planned to go back home for the first month of the two-month vacation, and come back to study for the second month. Students could choose among a number of courses to take in the summer at Wuhan University.

The idea of our returning for summer school was not so much to study, but to have more chances to be together. During the day we'd go to class, then spend some time studying, then we'd take a stroll together on the beautiful campus after dinner.

I thought of a poem on couples in love by Ouyang Xiu, from the 11th century, because it seemed to fit our lives perfectly.

The moon rises above the willows as couples meet after dusk.

Every morning when I woke up, I'd look forward to dusk as if my life existed for it. I longed to see Dongwei. Even so, in the first months, I'd intentionally be a bit late. This would demonstrate that I was

conservative and ladylike. A girl shouldn't seem too eager by always being exactly on time. Later, when we were more comfortable with each other, this kind of decorum was no longer necessary.

One evening, as with every other, we planned to meet at the little shady path around 7:30. When I arrived, however, Dongwei wasn't there.

I walked along the path for a little while, until I saw a slender man approaching me from behind. When I glanced back, he looked like Dongwei, so I stopped and waited for him. When he got closer, I realized to my dismay that it wasn't Dongwei. I felt embarrassed that I had waited for him.

"Are you here by yourself?" he asked, approaching me. "Which department are you from?"

"Sorry, I'm waiting for my boyfriend!" I replied hastily.

He laughed. "Is that me?"

I was embarrassed and anxious. I thought he must really think I was out hoping to meet a new boyfriend. Before I got angry, though, I realized it was perfectly reasonable if he thought that. Really, what else would a girl be doing out here by herself? I hurried back to my dorm.

By the time I got back, my anger at Dongwei was building inside me. Shouldn't he at least have let me know if he wasn't able to meet with me? Perhaps he was beginning to take me for granted.

I tried without success to calm down and study. I began reading a martial arts novel to distract myself.

Finally, around 11 p.m., someone knocked at my door. Standing there was a girl who lived in my building, from another department. She told me, "Your boyfriend has been waiting downstairs for you. He's been there for hours—I'm glad I bumped into him."

"Dongwei has been downstairs for hours?" A mix of emotions flooded me.

"Yes. He asked me if I could check to see if you're here. I'm amazed—he's so honest! There's no one watching the door, but he still wouldn't come up."

The school regulations stated that male students were prohibited from entering female dormitories. Every female dorm had a stern old lady who watched the door. The old ladies didn't work during the summer, but Dongwei still wouldn't break the rule.

I hurried downstairs. Seeing his anxious expression, all my anger evaporated.

He heaved a sigh of relief when he saw me, then he explained what had delayed him. "I bumped into my professor after dinner, and he was moving something heavy. I offered my help, so I was a little late. When I got to the path, I couldn't find you, so I came to look for you here. No one has come by here for hours. I'm so glad that girl came by."

I really wanted to scold him for being such a fool. Instead of waiting so long, he should have at least come up and knocked on my door.

At the same time, though, I was touched. I could definitely entrust myself to someone as honest as this.

The hundred-year-old Wuhan University campus is renowned for its beauty. Backed by Luojia Mountain, the campus faces the lovely East Lake, with undulating meadows in between. There are many green trees and fragrant flowers on the campus grounds.

My dorm was in the Garden of Sweet Osmanthus Flowers, as was

the party where Dongwei and I met. Just as its name implies, the garden was full of sweet osmanthus flowers, which were not particularly striking to look at, but in autumn when they bloomed, they gave off a mild, refreshing fragrance lasting a couple of months.

Dongwei studied biology, so his dorm was in the Garden of Cherry Blossoms. This garden has over a thousand cherry trees, many of which are the offspring of trees planted by Japanese soldiers to remind them of home during their occupation in 1938. There are those who are still embittered by the Japanese occupation and refuse to enjoy the trees. But regardless of their controversial origins, Cherry Blossom Road has become Wuhan University's landmark. In the spring, the road becomes a beautiful sea of blossoms, blanketing the trees, fluttering to the ground, swirling underfoot. Almost a million tourists come to see the display each year.

Dongwei and I first met in autumn, in the Garden of Sweet Osmanthus Flowers, and fell in love in the Garden of Cherry Blossoms in the spring. It was like living in a fairy tale.

———— • ————

With the grueling high school exams behind them, many students began to date for the first time in college. If Wuhan University's lovely, tranquil campus could talk, it could tell countless romantic love stories. It might also mention the many students who seemed to hop from one partner to another every couple of months.

I remember Dongwei talking to me about this. I hadn't actually noticed the phenomenon until he pointed it out. I myself had been influenced a little bit by the modern views emerging in China, but I also held many traditional ideas. I told him, "What happens now is what's important. What we become in the future depends on destiny. Why don't we continue this way for now, and see what happens?"

Dongwei did not like hearing this. He told me earnestly, "I'm serious when I have a girlfriend. I plan to marry her. If you only want to enjoy this moment, then let's just call it quits."

I felt hurt and indignant. How could he take me for one of those shallow girls who just wanted to have fun? I couldn't stand this injustice, and I replied hotly, "Fine, then! It's over!" and I stalked off.

Two days later, he came to see me and said that he could not stop feeling miserable. He wanted me to reconsider and treat our relationship seriously.

My indignation flared up again. How could he so easily dismiss my feelings toward him?

But I was also pleased. Because even if he did think that, at least he was miserable without me—he obviously still wanted to make it work. I got a very secure feeling about him, and we took a walk in the Garden of Cherry Blossoms and quickly made things right.

Dongwei had always wanted to be a scientist. So when he began to study at Wuhan University, he gave up the most popular profession at the time, computer science, in order to study genetics.

Even though Dongwei really loved the life sciences and excelled in them, he was still baffled by a lot of questions in this field.

I remember at the university, he came up with a great number of doubts about the theory of evolution.

He once told me, "According to the genetics we learned in class, mutation has a very low probability of occurring—about one in ten thousand, or even one in a billion. And by far most of the mutations are fatal. How likely is it that there could be enough mutations to bring about the evolutionary characteristics necessary to shape the species?"

He also doubted evolution because of a lack of supporting archaeological evidence. "If one life form can evolve into another, then why don't we see any transitional life forms?"

As a student of the arts, sometimes I would get bored listening to him talk about this sort of thing. Since I wasn't really able to understand all his objections, I would often brush him off. I'd say, "Don't think so much, just do well in your homework!"

He would reply, "You are so you. You don't pry any deeper than you need to. Think about it, if a house were about to collapse, what meaning would it have for the owners to start painting it and putting up wallpaper?"

Even though I did actually agree with him, I felt helpless in resolving such questions, and could only pretend to be interested.

Dongwei generally spoke in a pure, innocent, kind, and slightly childlike manner. I delighted in hearing him speak. Often I would stare at him without actually listening to what he was saying.

Sometimes he would realize I wasn't listening and say, "Oh, I see! You're ignoring me again!" So I would give him a kiss on the cheek and everything would be good again.

His doubts about evolution remind me of a conversation I had with a friend when I was seven or eight years old.

One day, my friend Juan came running up to me. "Do you know what? We come from apes!"

I immediately retorted, "I did not come from apes! I came from my mother's stomach. I have proof from the hospital."

She was stunned for a moment. "I came from my mother's stomach, too. Well, then it must be our mothers who came from apes."

I was very mad. "Probably your mother, but definitely not mine."

She still didn't know what to think, so we hurried to her house so she could ask her mother.

"Mom, did we come from apes?"

Juan's mother replied furiously, "Who said we came from apes?"

"My teacher."

Her mother softened a little. "Oh, I see. Well, that was a long time ago—not anymore now."

"Oh, I see," Juan nodded her head knowingly. "*Grandmother* came from apes."

Even when I grew up, I never did believe that humans had evolved from apes. But I still had no idea where we actually came from.

The origin of humans, and where humans are headed, became a great puzzle for me. My mind resonated with the words of Kahlil Gibran[1]:

> Only once have I been made mute. It was when a man asked me, "Who are you?"

Still, I reminded myself that other people didn't seem to be worried about such things. It didn't matter that much in my daily life, so I tried not to think about it.

Later, as Dongwei and I began to read articles on ancient civilizations such as ancient Athens and Egypt, we both became more and more interested. There was no way to explain the complex and varied cultures of those old civilizations from an evolutionary point of view. On the other hand, I was seeing strong evidence for the theory of periodic growth and destruction of civilizations.

Dongwei told me, "Even if just one of these findings is true, it will open up an entirely new field of science."

"Well," I said, "now that so many of these things have been discovered, why don't scientists open it up right now?"

After a moment of pondering, he muttered, "Yeah, why?"

———•———

In the late 1980s, something called *qigong*[2] had become popular. Wuhan University even had its own student Qigong Club, and would host seminars by all kinds of qigong masters.

Both Dongwei and I were interested in understanding

---

1   Kahlil Gibran, *Sand and Foam.* 1926

2   *qigong* (chee-gong)—a traditional Chinese exercise for balancing *qi*, or "life energy."

supernatural phenomena, and also hoped to find answers to some of our questions about life. We didn't miss a single qigong seminar.

Once, the Qigong Club at Huazhong Normal University in Wuhan hosted a *Shengsheng zhi yi* qigong seminar. We rode our bicycles to the seminar every night, a ride of 40 to 50 minutes.

I can't remember what the qigong master talked about, exactly. What I do remember is that he stirred up a major quarrel with the hosting club on the last day of class because he decided he wanted more money than they had originally agreed upon. The Qigong Club was comprised of young students, and in a fit of fury, the hosts declared that they would not charge any money for it at all.

All our money was refunded, and we lined up to get our refund while the qigong master stood red-faced nearby.

Because we were all poor college students, the tens of *yuan* at that time was not a small sum, but there was no joy in getting our money back. We felt really disappointed in this qigong master.

At the various seminars, we also saw a lot of examples of people using supernormal abilities. One time, the Qigong Club was playing a tape of a seminar given by a qigong master, Yan Xin. My roommate was there, and she was suddenly able to see things in other dimensions just by listening to the tape.

There was another time when two yoga masters from India arrived. We saw one of them levitate more than a meter above the ground. These things made us even more curious about qigong.

It was strange that the qigong masters themselves could not actually explain these phenomena and couldn't answer our questions. It was as though the phenomena just happened to them, and they didn't really understand why or how.

We weren't discouraged, though, because obviously there was something going on, and whatever it was, it was fascinating. We thought a qigong master might eventually show up who could answer our questions.

———•———

In February of 1988, we took a trip to Dongwei's parents' home for the Chinese New Year.

Dongwei is intelligent, and always did especially well in mathematics. On our trip, I discovered that in elementary and secondary school, he participated in mathematics competitions throughout the province and the nation, winning many awards.

For his accomplishments, he was given early admission to the Department of Biology in Wuhan University.

He had never mentioned any of this to me.

When we visited his alma mater, his teachers also told me about his academic excellence, his helpfulness, honesty, and courteousness. In the eyes of his teachers, Dongwei had been a model student and a role model for younger students. They implied that when I married him, it would be like winning the lottery.

I secretly winked at Dongwei when I heard some of these anecdotes and accolades. I thought it was wonderful—and I already felt I had won the lottery.

Still, I didn't completely value all these praises about Dongwei's honesty and good character. Though my mother had told me I still had to be a good person no matter what other people got away with, to me that didn't really mean I had to be perfectly honest at every moment. Small dishonesties when necessary were acceptable in my mind, and frankly I was a bit baffled by Dongwei's insistence that we always be completely forthright.

———— • ————

Dongwei is widely read and very knowledgeable. I could ask him questions about everyday life, and he would know the answers, such as why the moon is round, or how many teeth rabbits have. I gave him the nickname *Wan Shi Tong*, or "Little Encyclopedia."

Dongwei has had a thirst for knowledge since he was young. However, during the 1970s when we were growing up, the Cultural Revolution in China had eliminated or appropriated all spirituality from the Chinese people. Books were scarce, too. The only books Dongwei's parents ever bought him were a set of science books for children, called *Ten Thousand Whys*. There were 12 volumes in different subjects such as Biology, Chemistry, or the Earth. Over the years, he memorized everything in those books.

As the years progressed, however, he found that there were many questions he couldn't find in *Ten Thousand Whys*, and neither could he find the answers from anyone else.

Besides excelling in mathematics, Dongwei also had strong logical deduction skills. Unlike many people I knew, he didn't drown in the minutiae of a problem. Instead, he was able to see the larger picture.

He told me many times that, from probabilistic calculations, in this immense, varied, complex universe, from the largest to the most infinitely minute particles, there cannot exist only this three dimensional space that we experience. In the same way, the probability that Earth's humans are the only intelligent beings in this vast universe is also zero.

Dongwei also loved sports and painting when he was young, but he didn't accomplish much in these two areas when he grew older. He was left-handed as a child, but his parents and teachers forced him to use his right hand, which may have suppressed his sporting and artistic talents.

When he grew up, he became interested in photography, especially of nature. The pictures he took were perfect, and he developed a reputation for excellent photography among our small circle of friends and classmates.

When we would come across beautiful scenery on our holiday trips, both of us would shout excitedly, "Quick! Take a picture!"

Even though I didn't consider myself a classic beauty, I was more than willing to place myself in these beautiful photographs so we could enjoy the memories.

For him, though, he was crazy about scenery, and would always direct me, "Stand off to the side, don't block this tree." "Take a step back, your leg is still in the picture!"

When I pretended to get upset, he would start sweet-talking. "All right, all right, now let's do the real photos—I was only warming up

by taking a few scenery shots first."

When the pictures were developed, we would sit down and look at them together. We always had different ideas about which ones had turned out well. He never seemed to agree with me.

I asked him, "Why do our tastes in photos differ so much?"

"Because I look at the entire picture, and you're only looking at yourself—whether you look beautiful in that photo or not."

I thought about it and realized he was right.

Because we could only invite other people to take pictures of us together, the effect was never up to his standards. He regretted not being able to take photos of the two of us.

On our return from a trip to Donghu Lake when we were dating, Dongwei suddenly said, "Do you mind waiting before we have our first child?"

I was still too young and innocent to be thinking about the subject, and I turned as red as a tomato. I also felt a little annoyed, but stopped myself from blurting, "Who said I was going to marry you?" Instead, I asked, "Why?"

"Well, I heard that after you have little ones, your lifestyle changes completely and you end up stuck at home. We can enjoy life more if we have kids later."

At that time, I was still a bit immature and enjoyed my freedom. I couldn't imagine not having Dongwei for myself once we had a baby. But once we got our first jobs, we would find out how inaccurate our vision of the future had been. Life would not be as carefree and easy as we had imagined.

After graduation, each student was assigned a job and a city.

Although there were a lot of couples at the university, many wouldn't be able to stay together because they would be assigned to different cities. Distance and time would gradually erode their feelings for each other, and not many university relationships survived.

In the 1980s, students were usually assigned back to their hometown, so if the couple came from different provinces, it was very likely they would be separated. If they wanted to try to continue the relationship, one of them would apply with the city government for household registration in the city where the other lived. Many couples would wait ten years before their application was approved.

In theory, one of them could remain unemployed until the application was approved, but in practice, this was not feasible. Without both incomes, there was no way the couple could survive.

After graduating from his four-year program in 1989, Dongwei was assigned to a research institute in Zhengzhou City, Henan Province.

Fortunately, Dongwei and I both came from Xinxiang City, and I thought I might also be assigned to Zhengzhou, which was an hour away from Xinxiang. We would still be separated for a year while I finished school, but we always believed we could make it work.

While we were apart, we wrote letters every two or three days. After a year, we each had a thick bundle of them. I still vividly remember anticipating his letters, the thrill of receiving them, the joy in reading them, and countless nights spent writing to him.

When I graduated, I learned that I had indeed been assigned to Zhengzhou. The day Dongwei picked me up from the railway station, he gave me a big embrace, uncharacteristic for him in a public place, and smiling broadly, he said, "I'm so happy we're together again."

CHAPTER THREE

After many years of school, I thought employment would be a joyful thing, and I never expected we would have immediate financial problems.

When we were at the university, our families had been sending us funds. Actually, neither one of our families had much money, but they never let us know it. They tried their best to reduce their living expenses so they could send us enough money for college life. We didn't find this out until we got our first jobs.

I asked my father why he and my mother had sacrificed so much to send me the money. He said he never wanted me or my brother to live like he had in his youth.

In the early 1990s, the research institute where Dongwei worked paid only a small salary, which is typical for Chinese research organizations. He usually ran out of money days before the next paycheck because he would try to pay all our expenses when we went out together. He was not accustomed to living such a poor life.

Dongwei's college friends were in the same situation. One could not make money in this field in China. Many of his classmates had gone abroad, and most of the ones who remained in mainland China had changed professions.

Since I was working in the economics sector, I earned a higher salary than Dongwei. He made 100 yuan per month, and I made 400. It cost about 350 yuan to buy food, so there wasn't much left after that.

Dongwei didn't like letting me pay. But if I hadn't been working, we wouldn't have been able to survive. As a long-term solution, we decided to apply for graduate school in Beijing.

Dongwei decided to study international trade, hoping we could live better after graduation. He actually preferred the life science subjects, but he realized it would be hard to find a well-paying job in that field.

For the same reason, I chose a somewhat popular major, finance, for my graduate studies. We were quite happy to return to school and get away from the difficulties of work life. Our parents understood the financial situation we faced, so they were willing to support us through another round of college.

———•———

Housing is a huge problem in China, especially for people like us who had moved from external provinces to Beijing.

One day in June of 1995, just before we completed our master's programs, Dongwei suddenly said to me, "Let's get married!"

We had been dating for eight years, and my heart could not help but pound when I heard that. I lowered my head in embarrassment and waited for him to recite a romantic proposal.

"That way," he said, "once we start working, we can get in line for an apartment."

I looked up at him, ready to burst out in anger, but when I saw the innocence in his eyes, I changed my mind.

"Fine then," I retorted. "We can queue up at the same time, and get a bigger place."

Thus, we were finally married.

Chinese people say "It takes ten years of cultivation for two people to sit on the same boat, and it takes a hundred years of cultivation for them to become husband and wife." That is, for two people to have such a strong tie, they must have gone through a lot together in past lives.

When we began dating, I was only 17 and he was 18. Most people thought our relationship wouldn't last, that we were just having fun. I was delighted to prove them wrong.

Some classmates used to tell us, "You two have dated for so long. Your feelings for each other will likely subside once you get married."

To many people, "toning down" is a phrase that does not bode well for love and marriage. Not only does it suggest an insipid life, it is also the main excuse for extra-marital affairs.

Sometimes we would fight, and like other girls I knew, I would occasionally threaten him with divorce.

Every time I would mention divorce, the good-tempered Dongwei would suddenly become angry.

"Speak logic and reason—don't speak such nonsense!" His voice would be clear and resounding.

Seeing him so solemn, I would know I'd gone too far, and I would immediately stop.

One day, I playfully pondered which of us loved the other more. I said that I loved him more, and he said that he loved me more. At one point he stopped being playful and said, "I don't know, there's no

way to measure it. But I do know that if two people decide to spend their entire lives together, there should be no talk of parting."

———— • ————

After graduation, we were both able to find decent jobs in Beijing. I became a credit analyst of a state-owned bank, and Dongwei worked in a big international trade company.

They were white-collar, high-income jobs by standards in China at the time, and the work environment was good. After work, we would often go out to eat, meet friends, or watch a movie or performance.

In the past, when we were poor students, we had to walk or bike long distances whenever we wanted to go anywhere, to save money on public transportation. Now that we were both well-paid, we thought we should be happy because things were so much easier.

We should have been perfectly content. But we were beginning to discover that raising one's standard of living does not address all the needs of an individual. Without taking one's spiritual needs into account, it is difficult to lead a truly happy life.

My biggest material concern was housing. In China, only high officials, movie stars, and successful entrepreneurs can afford to buy houses. Most of the working people live in apartments. In the 1990s, the cost of buying a two-bedroom apartment in Beijing was about 20 times our yearly salaries. Loans were not easy to get, and 30 percent of the amount was required for the down payment. The only chance we had to live in our own apartment was to get one from the state-owned companies we worked for. In that case, the workplace would provide the apartment without charge, as part of our employment compensation.

Since 1949, most Chinese people have worked for state-owned companies, factories, or in the government, and receive a subsistence salary, enough only for food, clothes, and some basic necessities. Housing and health care are allocated to employees by state-owned work units, but there are not enough apartments or health care to go around. People have to fight with each other to obtain them.

No fixed standard was set up when allocating these benefits. The work unit might choose recipients based on age, work experience, marital status, or sometimes by level of education. Often, leaders would give apartments to their own family members and friends first.

At the end of 1995, the year we began working in Beijing, my parents were both asked to retire from their workplace—the same place in which they had met 27 years earlier. Their factory was in a slump, so it forced employees 50 years and older to retire. They were given a small retirement income.

Because their housing conditions were bad, my parents wanted to come and live with us. The tradition in China is for each generation to help the other, and there is an expectation that children will help their parents when they begin to earn a living. In addition, my parents were very fond of us.

Of course we had no place for them. My brother was still in college, so the responsibility really fell to me. They had worked so hard all their lives—I wanted them to be able to relax now and enjoy life.

At that time, Dongwei and I lived in a 430-square-foot, one-bedroom apartment shared with another young couple. The apartment and the couple had been assigned to us by Dongwei's workplace. He and the young man were colleagues.

Because Dongwei was older, we took the bedroom and they got the living room. We had to pass by the living room to get to the rest of the place, so they hung up a piece of thick cloth to separate their area. We also tried to stay in our room as much as possible, to allow them a semblance of privacy.

My mother called me from time to time to ask when we would get our own apartment so she and my father could move in. It was already stressful sharing that tiny apartment, and the pressure from my parents added to my mental burden.

————•————

One day in March of 1996, when I called my mother, she seemed quite delighted. She told me that recently she and my father had gone to a nearby park looking for a good qigong practice for healing and fitness.

There were several kinds of qigong being practiced in the park, so they looked for the group that had the most people in it. That's how they found *Falun Gong*. My mother told me that the practice had had a dramatic effect on her health, and they both wanted me to read the Falun Gong book.

I really liked the idea of something supernormal, and I liked that my parents were enthusiastic about something. But I had just started a new job and was especially busy. I told her not to send it yet, but to give it to me the next time I visited.

For the next six months, my mother repeatedly told me about the benefits of Falun Gong, also called *Falun Dafa*.[3] I felt happy for her, and also somehow relieved. Because if my parents were doing well, that meant it wasn't so urgent to get our own apartment for them.

———•———

In September, I was finally able to take a vacation, so I went to visit my parents in Xinxiang.

Walking into the house, everything seemed a little different, but I couldn't pinpoint exactly what it was. After the first half a day, I realized what the difference was—it was my mother.

My mother had always had frail health, and always had this or that medical issue. Because she lost her parents as a child, she was timid and sensitive and was often bullied by others. Every time I went home to see her, she was either in bed recuperating from some incident, or the entire visit would consist of her enumerating her grievances and injustices.

This time, when I entered the house, she was sitting at her sewing machine, sewing something. I sat on the sofa beside her and gazed into her face, finding it amazingly calm. Then she asked me about my life and my job, all the while working quietly on her sewing. Something was different. Something was strange. All of a sudden I realized what it was—she hadn't made a single complaint!

Later, I pulled out some medicine I brought for her from Beijing, as I always did.

She smiled. "Thanks, but you don't have to buy me any more of that. My illness is completely gone. I've thrown away all my medicine."

She'd thrown away her medicine? Over the phone, she had told me that her illnesses had been cured by practicing Falun Dafa, but I never believed it. I thought she just felt somewhat better and was trying to comfort me. But apparently it had really happened! In China, medical expenses are quite a burden for most people. I knew she wouldn't have thrown her medicine away if she might need it at some point. I was overjoyed.

A little while later, to my surprise, I found that my father's temper had also improved.

In China, we have an old saying. "Rivers and mountains can

---

3   *Falun Dafa*—can be translated as "Law-Wheel Great-Law." It is a unique qigong practice that cultivates a Law-Wheel in the lower abdomen instead of a *dan*, or elixer. "*Gong*" refers to high level cultivation energy, and is more powerful than qi.

change, but people's character will remain." This trip was a miracle! So of course I brought the book *Zhuan Falun*[4] back with me to Beijing.

When I got home, I read the first two pages, the introduction. I was immediately stunned. I felt it was deeply profound, and I somehow had the feeling this book would answer all the problems in my life. But unfortunately, I had to catch up on work after my vacation, so I closed the book and put it on a shelf.

About two weeks later, one of Dongwei's colleagues told me that his company had recently acquired some new apartments. Naturally, there were a lot of people fighting to get them. Dongwei and I were a married couple, but we didn't have much work experience, so it was unlikely we would be considered for a housing allocation.

Dongwei's colleague suggested to me that we give the manager in the housing department some gifts in order to have a higher chance of getting a house.

I told Dongwei about this advice. He said he was not used to doing such things. "We should leave it to fate," he said.

I immediately flared up. "Well, who does like to do such things? Not everyone has a choice, you know! Why don't you go and be your own uncorrupted person—by yourself!"

He happened to be on his way out the door. Usually when he had to go somewhere, he would say a few kind words to me, such as, "Stay safely at home, okay? Cook something for yourself, don't just eat junk food." Then he'd give me a hug.

This time he said nothing. He simply left.

I was miserable. I couldn't bring myself to do anything useful, so I slumped down on the floor of our bedroom. I covered my face with my hands and sighed about the hardships and pains in life.

As I sat there, all of a sudden a thought flashed into my mind. It said, "Why don't you take a look at that book now?"

I walked over and took out the book, sat in front of the window, and began to read.

I kept reading and reading, for eight or nine hours. Everything around me stopped, and I sat motionless until I finished the book. I never even thought about eating or drinking.

In those eight or nine hours, I felt that I had risen above countless layers of the universe and undergone countless incarnations. Only

---

4   *Zhuan Falun*—"Turning the Law-Wheel."

after I finished reading and closed the book did I feel I had returned to the human realm.

I sat there, struck and stunned, yet peaceful inside.

I felt that the book had explained all the unresolved puzzles throughout history, science and the human world. Teacher Li[5] said in the book that people would have this reaction—my entire view of the world had changed.

All of a sudden, I felt I had been enlightened to the real purpose in life—to return to my original, true self by cultivating spiritual perfection. I knew how I should handle myself from that point on.

That night when I was sleeping, a storm raged in my mind. In my dreams I saw countless scenes and went through a major transformation. When I woke, I couldn't remember any of the details.

The next day, I strongly recommended to Dongwei that he read it. He said that he was too busy right then.

This lasted for a week until I became really impatient. "I missed out on this book for two weeks for the same reason as you—I was too busy. Now I really regret it! You don't know how much you're missing out on every day."

When he saw how serious I was, he replied, "Actually I've already prepared to take some time to read the book. Do you know why?"

I shook my head.

"Have you noticed?" he said. "You haven't mentioned anything about housing problems for a whole week! I have to read this book and see what made you change your mind."

So he began reading *Zhuan Falun*.

When he finished the book, all his doubts and questions about science were answered perfectly.

"So we should cultivate together, yes?" I asked impatiently.

"Of course," he said.

I heaved a sigh of relief. If he had been opposed to it, I'd planned to say I wanted a divorce, to try to get him to change his mind.

After we started cultivating, though, I never wanted to bring up that word again. Falun Gong teaches *Zhen-Shan-Ren*,[6] or

5   This refers to Mr. Li Hongzhi, who introduced Falun Gong to the public in 1992. Practitioners of Falun Gong often refer to him as Teacher Li or Master Li as a form of respect and in keeping with traditional customs in martial arts and cultivation circles.

6   Chinese words often have complex meanings. *Zhen* can be translated as truth, truthfulness, or being true. *Shan* can be compassion, kindness, goodness, or benevolence. *Ren* can be forbearance, tolerance, or endurance, and includes things such as patience, fortitude, and self-control.

Truthfulness, Compassion, and Tolerance. Saying I wanted a divorce would have violated all three principles.

Falun Gong is a cultivation practice that improves both mind and body. Besides cultivating one's character according to the principles of *Zhen-Shan-Ren*, there are also physical movements, in the form of five exercises.

One day I asked my colleagues, "Do you know of any Falun Gong practice sites nearby where we can learn the exercises?"

"Oh, Falun Gong? Just go to any park in the morning, you'll definitely find them. They're everywhere."

I was filled with joy. It was wonderful that there were so many people studying this.

At that time, we lived near the Asia Sports Village in Beijing. In the morning, we hurried to the local park and indeed saw 20 or 30 people practicing there.

The calm, soothing music brought tranquility to my heart. Everyone was practicing silently. We saw an older woman, about 50 years old, standing to the side and watching everyone with a kind expression on her face. We figured she must be the local site coordinator we had read about.

She saw us and smiled. "Do you want to learn Falun Gong? We teach free of charge."

Upon obtaining such a precious practice method, I was willing to give everything I had to show my respect. I replied anxiously, "Is there any practice site that charges a fee? I want to pay."

The lady laughed. "No, dear. Our Teacher has come to teach us how to be good people, and we are not allowed to use the practice to earn money."

Falun Dafa was free of charge, yet its health benefits were much better than anything we'd tried before. Dongwei used to have stomach problems, and he could not eat cold food. After he started practicing Falun Dafa, the problems disappeared and he could grab things to eat directly out of the fridge.

Soon we wanted to share our joy with friends and colleagues. I recommended *Zhuan Falun* to a good friend, and after reading it, she could not stop exclaiming, "This is too good to be true!" She became a cultivator herself.

At that time, *Zhuan Falun* was sold in bookstores everywhere. It was the number one bestseller in Beijing in 1996.

My husband was always a simple and easygoing person, and it seemed to me that he was without grand ambitions. His original desire was to be a scientist. However, as he grew older and took more science classes, he realized that science was unlike what he had envisioned, so he gave up this ambition.

After graduating from graduate school in Beijing, he accepted a position in a big import-export company.

Once in a while I would ask him, "Now that you're in business, don't you want to become a big businessman and own a big company?"

He'd reply, "Well, if I'm working and the money comes naturally, then that's great. But if you're saying I should be unscrupulous, there's no way I'm going to do that."

At the time, I was filled with the materialistic desires of a young girl. I said, "But I really need money. You have to do everything possible to get it!" He knew I was joking, but he did also feel some pressure from this.

After cultivating in Falun Dafa, I no longer believed that his lack of passion for wealth was a flaw. I realized it was actually a good thing not to absorb oneself in material desires all the time. I also realized that honesty is a quality people should have, and I finally began to see the goodness in Dongwei's character.

He told me after we started cultivating that he was deeply relieved that I no longer mentioned the importance of pursuing wealth. He said he had actually been worried that I might run away with a wealthy man one day if he failed to earn enough money.

I was indignant. "What kind of person do you think I am? So I was a bit materialistic. Do you think I would have stooped that low?"

"I couldn't really tell for sure," he replied seriously. "Look at the direction society is going. A lot of girls who used to be really good later became infatuated with the idea of money, didn't they?"

Conversely, I should say that before he started cultivating in Falun Dafa, Dongwei's lack of interest in money was also mixed with some passivity and antipathy toward the world. But after starting cultivation, he saw that one has to be a good person in everything one does. So he developed a more vivacious attitude toward life. He put in more effort and took more responsibility at work.

Our financial situation improved a lot.

———— • ————

One day, Dongwei and I were wandering around the city, shopping for furniture, when we were approached by a beautiful girl in her twenties, asking for directions. Dongwei began telling her the way very patiently. After a while, I thought, "This is beyond ordinary patience."

When he first started talking to her, I was happy to see him being so courteous, but after several minutes, I became uncomfortable. I stood anxiously waiting for him to stop talking to her.

Finally I thought, "That's just fine. I'm going to ignore you for the next couple of days. We'll see if you ever flirt with another girl again!"

I ignored him for several minutes, but alas, he never noticed.

Then we met another person asking for directions on the road. This time it was a poor laborer around 40 years old. Dongwei spoke to him with exactly the same patient manner he had used with the beautiful girl, and even ended up walking him to his destination. It was obvious to me now that he hadn't been flirting with the woman. Apparently I had been the one with the problem.

———◆———

Dongwei's views on romantic love had always differed greatly from mine. I've always liked reading love stories and hoped Dongwei would read them with me so we could discuss them together. But he felt those books were too artificial and thought it was silly to discuss them.

I forced him to read them anyway. He ended up confusing the characters in different stories after reading only two books, and asked me why the boy in this story loves the girl in the other book.

But Dongwei was actually rather romantic in other ways. He could remember all the important anniversaries in our relationship—the first day we met, our first date, the day we first held hands.

He would give me a delicate gift for my birthday, after which I would say, "Next time, please ask me what I want."

"You're such a wet blanket. I wanted to give you a surprise."

I always thought it would be the most romantic thing if he recited love poems from the ancient Chinese book, *The Book of Poetry*. I imagined that I would stand by the window and he would recite romantically:

Born after death, meet and separate, I have talked with you,
Hand-in-hand, till death do us part.

I would turn and reply:

> *At first, when we set out, the willows were fresh and green,*
> *Now, when we shall be returning, the snow will be falling in clouds.*[7]

But every time I suggested such a thing, he would laugh out loud, saying, "There's no way I could do it. I wouldn't be able to stop laughing!"

————•————

After we began to cultivate in Falun Gong, our life became simple and joyful. In our work and everyday life, we conducted ourselves according to our practice—according to the principles of Truthfulness, Compassion, and Tolerance. Our days were fulfilling, and our physical and spiritual health improved.

Every night, including weekends, Dongwei and I studied *Zhuan Falun* together at home. Sometimes I would pause and glance at him, and when I saw him studying so attentively, I would smile and continue reading.

If he discovered me looking at him, he might say, "You're not studying the book very well! Your punishment will be to cook dinner tonight!"

He was just kidding, though. Who knows what the meal would have tasted like if I cooked it. So I would always prep the food, and he would cook it. Fortunately one of us was a good cook.

Every weekend we went to the park to practice the exercises. Then we strolled in the shade just like we used to do in our university days, and talked about our cultivation experiences. It was a beautiful and unforgettable time.

————•————

Even though a great deal of traditional Chinese culture was destroyed during the Cultural Revolution, the Chinese people have a long tradition in Buddhism and Taoism. Even today, Chinese people are still familiar with the idea of cultivation practice.

Chinese history and culture abound with stories about cultivation in Buddhism and Taoism that everyone knows, such as The Eight Immortals, Monk Jigong, and Monk Bu Dai.

But only after we began our cultivation in Falun Gong did we

---

7   2nd stanza: Minor odes of the kingdom, Decade of Lu Ming. *Cai Wei*. Trans. James Legge

truly realize that the ancient practice of cultivating is not mythology, nor is it philosophy, theory, or doctrine. And it's definitely not just exercises. Cultivation in Falun Dafa is a path that reveals the true meaning of life and provides a way to return to one's true self.

Practicing Falun Dafa is simpler than most cultivation methods because it has no special location or format, such as entering a cave or monastery. Dongwei and I were able to cultivate while working at our jobs and going about our everyday lives, simply by living according to the principles of Truthfulness, Compassion, and Tolerance.

Cultivation cleansed our physical bodies as well as our spirits, and we could see ourselves improving.

At that time, Dongwei was mainly in charge of foreign exports at work. Through business negotiations, he often came across situations in which customers wanted him to drink or smoke with them.

This was becoming an issue for him because he didn't want to be unsociable, but on the other hand he really wanted to honor the requirement that a cultivator should not drink alcohol or smoke.

In his early days of cultivation, he often said he was going to be driving, so he shouldn't drink. After a while we discussed this, and realized this excuse wasn't really true. So he decided to tell his customers that as a Falun Gong cultivator, he has to adhere to the requirements of cultivation, which means not drinking.

We realized that not until Dongwei started telling the truth did it fundamentally resolve the problem. From that time on, whenever someone offered him a drink, another colleague would say, "He practices Falun Gong, so he doesn't drink."

In the business world of today's China, it is common for business partners to give and receive gifts. This kind of gift-giving is actually a way of encouraging someone to do things in your favor—for example, my previous desire to give gifts to the housing manager in Dongwei's company in hopes of getting an apartment.

Dongwei's customers often wanted to give him gifts, but as cultivators, we decided not to accept them anymore. He was already earning a salary, and it didn't feel right to get something extra for doing what was just part of his job.

Sometimes his customers gave him gifts that were intended for me, his wife, such as bracelets or handbags. Some of the things were quite lovely. Even though I always politely refused the gifts, I couldn't help but stare at them for a moment.

Dongwei would see my reaction, and on our way home he would

always gently suggest, "Let's go buy it ourselves if we want it, okay?"

———————•———————

Not long after we began practicing Falun Gong, our workplace allocated us a rather ideal house. Finally, we had a home!

The place was a newly built condominium and wasn't quite finished. Neither Dongwei nor I had time to do the work ourselves, so we hired a contractor who said he could have the work completed in two months.

The plans were quite simple, so we had no concerns about turning the key over to the person in charge of the work.

A month later, a colleague told me, "When my place was being built, I watched the contractors every day. They weren't doing their job and they were using substandard materials. You shouldn't give them too much freedom if you want the job done correctly."

I smiled and said, "Wow, is it that bad? All right, I'd better go have a look."

After lunch I took a taxi to the new place. When I entered, I was dumbstruck.

A whole gang of workers was eating lunch in the living room, and the room was filled with utensils and beds. There was no sign of any work having been completed whatsoever. When they saw me enter, they all stood up in surprise.

I tried to compose myself and said, "There are so many people here—are you all working on this one house? Why doesn't it look like anything's been done?"

One young worker explained, "We're working on a number of condos in this area, and we're living in this one. Our manager told us to finish the others first, before this one. Otherwise we wouldn't have anywhere to stay."

I couldn't believe it. They were using our house as a hostel, and not even doing any work for us!

On my way back to work, I called Dongwei and asked him to talk to the building company's boss that night.

During the entire afternoon, I ranted and seethed. My colleagues agreed with me. "Look at people nowadays," they said. "Can you trust them to do anything good for you without monitoring them constantly? You're so foolish to have trusted them. How could anyone be so stupid?"

After work, Dongwei came to look for me, and we went to the new house to find the manager. Along the way, he saw my frustration and comforted me. "When I first heard this, I was pretty angry too, but later I remembered Teacher's words in *Zhuan Falun* and felt much better. Do you remember?"

He recited back to me a section from the book's fourth lecture.

As practitioners, you will suddenly come across conflicts. What should you do? You should always maintain a heart of compassion and kindness. Then, when you run into a problem, you will be able to do well because it gives you room to buffer the confrontation. You should always be benevolent and kind to others, and consider others when doing anything. Whenever you encounter a problem, you should first consider whether others can put up with this matter or if it will hurt anyone. In doing so, there will not be any problems. Therefore, in cultivation practice you should follow a higher and higher standard for yourself.[8]

It was miraculous. Hearing him say those words extinguished all the raging fury in my heart like a fountain of cool water. I calmed down and relaxed immediately. As I thought about it further, I realized it was really nothing to make a fuss about since those workers were in a bad situation as well.

When we reached the building, the manager began apologizing profusely. He told us they would start working on it immediately and would definitely complete the project on time.

I thought since there was not much time left, how could they complete it on time without the workers working day and night? Our Teacher taught us to be considerate of others, so I said, "It's all right if it's not done on time. We just want it to be done well."

The manager never considered that we'd be so understanding and calm. He asked, "Are you two religious?"

We were shocked by his question and said, "Yes, we are spiritual and we practice Falun Gong. How did you know?"

The manager replied, "Oh, Falun Gong, of course! You know, everyone nowadays is always scheming, trying to get hold of something, and then if they do, they're afraid they'll lose it. I hardly ever see anyone as understanding as you two."

———•———

Once we started cultivating, our troubles no longer revolved around our difficulties and achievements at work and in life, or the harms inflicted

8   Li Hongzhi, *Zhuan Falun*. (Taipei, Taiwan: Yin Chyun, 2002), 162-3

on us by others. Instead, our concerns were about how we hadn't done so well in certain situations, and how we might better adhere to the principles of Truthfulness, Compassion, and Tolerance.

As I practiced more, my heart became peaceful and tranquil. There seemed to be a glass wall separating me from ordinary fights over personal benefits. To others, it was an invisible wall, but to me, it was solid and impenetrable. The tranquility in my heart was beyond what I could have expected.

Both of us excelled at our work, and our lives improved tremendously.

———•———

Dongwei had always been a good son to his parents, a good husband to his wife, and a good student for his teachers. After cultivating, the compassion and purity hidden inside him were revealed ever more clearly. As a result, I also developed a deeper sense of respect for him alongside our love. Some of the things Dongwei accomplished really amazed me.

We donated money toward forest restoration projects in western areas of China, and we helped a total of nine children in faraway provinces to go to school, through "Project Hope." At that time, our income was above average in China, and to donate some money was not a problem for us.

Every year in September, at the start of school, Dongwei would buy pencils, exercise books, and dictionaries so that he could send them to children in rural areas. He was afraid their studies would be disrupted if they didn't have the money to buy such things.

Then, during the New Year, he would buy calendars, pencil cases, and other things and send them to the children as gifts, to share a portion of our New Year's happiness with them.

Although these children were far away in different provinces, they regarded Dongwei as a part of their family. They would report their study results regularly, and sometimes they would send various local food products to "Uncle Dongwei."

Once, a child from Inner Mongolia sent us his mother's homemade rice biscuits. For some reason, by the time they arrived, the biscuits were as hard as rocks. I suggested we throw them away to protect our teeth.

Yet Dongwei said, "Those biscuits are gifts from the children. Let's try to dunk them and see if they can be softened."

In the mornings that followed, Dongwei ate the dunked biscuits for breakfast but never allowed me to share them with him. I could only imagine how they must have tasted.

———◆———

When we first started cultivating in Falun Dafa, Dongwei was 28 years old and I was 27. It was the peak of our lives and we got tremendous energy from practicing.

We were competent at our jobs and praised by our supervisors and colleagues—we both rose rapidly into important work positions. However, because we were so busy with work, we could only go to the park to practice the exercises on the weekends.

Our new home was close to Purple Bamboo Park, which is one of the seven largest parks in Beijing. At that time, the Peony Pavilion in the park had a large practice site.

We were among the first to practice there, with more than a hundred other practitioners. More and more people joined as time went by, until it was so crowded that two more practice sites were started at the east and west gates of the park. Soon the new practice sites also had one to two hundred people each.

When we did the exercises with so many other practitioners, we felt very light and spirited.

———◆———

After moving into our new home, we began making plans to have a baby.

I learned from a book that it was easier to care for a baby born in May, because of the mild temperature.

When I told Dongwei about this, he just laughed at me. "If all the babies were born in May, how busy the hospital would be! And it would be so dull if everyone's birthday was celebrated in May!"

"All right," I said. "We can follow the natural path if you want—but I hope the baby won't be born in the dead of winter."

We thought our beautiful life could last, but after the persecution began, everything would turn upside-down. Our daughter would not come in 1999 as we had originally planned, but more than five years later—as a surprise, during a severe January.

CHAPTER FOUR

In 1996, when we first began the practice, there were approximately 20 million practitioners. By 1998, there were already 70 million. Since Falun Gong has tremendous benefits for one's health and moral values, its popularity required no help from advertisements. It spread from person to person, especially among family members. It was like Teacher Li said in an interview in Australia on May 2, 1999:

> I believe that this Dafa practice is a serious thing. Singing its praises in various media, as if doing advertising, wouldn't be serious, though, and so we haven't done such things in print media. Basically, students share news with their family and friends of their general well being, talking about their heartfelt feelings and how their health has improved, or how after learning the teachings of Falun Gong they are drawn to them. We wouldn't lie to our own family or spouse about this kind of thing, so what is said has to be true, people realize. You would never entice your own wife or kids, or family or friends to follow suit after you were duped by something. That doesn't happen.

I saw this figure of 70 million practitioners in an article in the Zaobao newspaper in Singapore. At that time, my job was to analyze international financial markets to identify trends and risks, so I often read foreign media and visited foreign websites. Before 1999, the large-scale Internet blockade had not yet been instated, and one could still see a lot of information on the web.

The Zaobao article said that statistics from the Public Security Department of the People's Republic of China (PRC) held that there were approximately 70 million Falun Gong practitioners throughout the country. They also stated that Falun Gong practitioners outnumbered Communist Party members.

I was not surprised when I saw the 70 million figure. We saw how the number of practitioners in our practice site had grown, and I knew for sure that more and more people would come to learn. But I did feel uncomfortable with the article's comment about Falun Gong practitioners outnumbering Communist Party members.

Falun Gong is a cultivation practice and is comprised of cultivators. The Chinese Communist Party is a political party, and a lot of Party members and government officials had actually become Falun Gong practitioners as well. Falun Gong and the CCP are not even parallel entities. It would be equally pointless to state that in the United States, Christians outnumber Republican Party members.

Later I found out that as early as 1997 and 1998, some Communist Party officials had already decided they would label Falun Gong a "cult" and persecute its practitioners in order to elevate themselves politically. It's probably because of this that they conducted such comparisons, in order to prepare excuses for the coming persecution.

——◆——

In early 1999, Dongwei and I went every Saturday afternoon to a Falun Dafa study group. Seven or eight practitioners in our neighborhood would gather to read *Zhuan Falun* for two hours or so. Then people would share about how they were trying to live their lives according to the principles of *Zhen-Shan-Ren*, and about how the principles had improved their character.

When we gathered together to share experiences, topics like how to fight for personal gain never entered the discussion. We all talked about how we could improve, and areas in which we had not been able to adhere to the principles, how we had overcome obstacles in our cultivation path, and how we had managed to rid ourselves of bad thoughts and actions.

It was a golden time because we were able to study and compare with other practitioners to find our flaws. Improvement was rapid.

In our study group, there was a girl around our age named Yang Yan, who was straightforward and outgoing. Soon after I met her, we became good friends.

She had graduated from Peking University with a degree in Chinese Language and was working in the Law Section of the Beijing Economic and Trade Committee. During that time, she always wore a Falun Gong pin, which resembled a beautiful flower, near her chest pocket.

I asked, "Do you wear it at work too?"

She nodded. "I wear it every day, so I am always reminded that I'm a Falun Dafa cultivator and that I mustn't do anything that goes against *Zhen-Shan-Ren*. Why don't you wear one too?"

"I don't dare to," I said, "because I don't think I've cultivated very well. Sometimes I can't control myself, and I get angry. Wouldn't I disgrace Falun Gong if I wore it?"

She replied sincerely, "Then you must be stricter with yourself!"

I nodded, and felt my face flush.

———•———

In early 1999, the bank where I worked was bought by a larger bank, and many people at my workplace used this opportunity to change jobs and work in a foreign bank.

According to the regulations in Beijing, a citizen from another city would not be allowed to work in a foreign bank in Beijing without first becoming a Beijing resident. Only students originally from Beijing could go directly to work in a foreign bank after graduation.

Therefore, a lot of people began by working in state-owned banks in Beijing so they could get their registration permit there before switching jobs if the opportunity should arise. I was already a manager at that time and it would have been fairly easy for me to get a much better job in a foreign bank, but I didn't.

There were many reasons why I didn't make the switch, but one of the most important was that someone told me there were dozens of Falun Gong practitioners who worked at the bank that had bought ours, and many of them gathered to practice the exercises in the multi-purpose room during the lunch break.

I was thrilled. Normally, I didn't have time to practice the exercises in the park on weekday mornings. Now I could practice at noon.

———•———

In early 1999, certain domestic media reported that the number of Falun Gong practitioners was already up to one hundred million. *Zhuan Falun* had been translated to many foreign languages and had been spread in over 30 countries and regions all over the world. Some Westerners even came to China to learn Chinese so they could read the original Chinese version of *Zhuan Falun*.

As more and more people began practicing Falun Gong, I was as happy as a bird and thought what a wonderful practice this is that can help people remove their illnesses, save on medical expenses, and teach people to have compassion in their hearts. Cultivating Falun Gong has a hundred benefits and does no harm.

That's why I was completely confused when, for the first time, I heard that someone was afraid of practicing it.

This woman was a former colleague of mine, and she had been diagnosed with a uterine tumor. No medicine had worked for her, and she was not willing to undergo surgery. I recommended that she practice Falun Gong. She started to practice it, and was delighted when the pains in her abdomen disappeared.

Later, I brought her with me to join a large group exercise activity at Capital Stadium. Practitioners from Haidian District held the exercises outside the stadium one weekend per month, and sometimes there were so many practitioners they wouldn't all fit on the stadium square.

When we got there, we saw the spectacle of thousands of people practicing the exercises together, with vivid banners hung around the square, saying "Falun Dafa, Free Instruction."

I was marveling at the sight when my friend suddenly said, "Oh, my God!" There was fear in her voice. "I didn't know there were so many people practicing this! I want to go home now. I'm not going to practice this anymore."

"What?" I was dumbfounded.

She shook her head emphatically. "The CCP will never allow this many people to practice!" She quickly left.

I was confused by her odd behavior.

Later on, I heard that her illness had returned. In the end, she went to the hospital for surgery, and it took a long time for her to recover.

I shared her case with other practitioners in our group, and they all felt it was a pity that she missed out on such a good practice. Of course we couldn't push her to resume practicing. No matter how much we cherished this precious opportunity, she had to decide for herself.

April 24, 1999, was a Saturday. As usual that afternoon, we studied the book *Zhuan Falun* and shared our understandings with each other. Near the end of the evening, an older female practitioner joined us with some news.

She told us that the day before, some policemen from Tianjin, a city close to Beijing, had beaten Falun Gong practitioners. The practitioners had gone there to explain the nature of Falun Gong to an editor of a magazine who had published something negative about the practice. In addition to the beatings, the police also detained more than 40 practitioners.

The Tianjin Police claimed they were just following orders from their superiors. They told the practitioners to go to Beijing and appeal to the higher authorities for help.

So the members of our study group discussed whether we should go and appeal. Since we ourselves lived in Beijing, we thought it made sense that we should go. Most of us agreed to go the following day, except for a few practitioners who had other commitments.

With this thought, very early in the morning on April 25, we went to the Appeals Office of the State Council, located on Fuyou Street on the west side of Zhongnanhai. We felt it was natural to express our opinion to the government, and since many people were involved, we went there together.

This was the "Peaceful Appeal at Zhongnanhai on April 25, 1999," that shocked the world.

All the practitioners lined up by the street, leaving enough walking space for pedestrians and not interfering with cars. So as not to disturb the local residents who were using the very limited public restrooms nearby, most of the practitioners neither ate nor drank anything the whole day.

Nothing happened until it started getting dark. Dongwei and I had to work early the next morning, so we left earlier than most people.

In the evening, we heard that the higher officials had learned about our problem, and Prime Minister Zhu Rongji had already authorized the Tianjin police to release the detained practitioners. He also promised to take into account the request made by the representative practitioners to end the harassment of Falun Gong.

The practitioners left in a good mood after hearing that. We heard that the last group of practitioners cleaned the ground carefully without leaving even a scrap of paper behind.

Some of the top officials in the CCP Central Committee were

astounded by this event, thinking that Falun Gong practitioners must have a tight organizational network and tough discipline. There had been many protests in China over the years, but they were never peaceful and orderly. Respectful, harmonious behavior was unprecedented. But for Falun Gong practitioners it was quite natural. No one had to organize or discipline this huge group. It was the result of their assimilating to the principles of Truthfulness, Compassion, and Tolerance, without the need for exterior discipline.

On Monday morning, all my colleagues in the office were talking about the "4/25 event." From listening to them, it sounded like it had been no simple event.

I told them I had been there.

They were all astonished and said, "Oh, my God! You went there, too?! You better not participate in that from now on."

I laughed upon hearing this and said, "We just went there to tell the officials our situation. It is not as serious as you imagine."

One of my colleagues shook his head. "You are really naïve! You'll find out soon enough. In China, there are some matters you should never, ever get involved in. If you do, you'll end up in a lot of trouble."

I refused to take it seriously no matter how much fuss they made. In my mind, it was a good thing for people to express their opinions, especially in such a peaceful way.

But my older colleagues had personally experienced many movements started by the CCP, and they well knew how the Party controls the Chinese people—with violence and lies.

———— ♦ ————

Shortly after the incident, some strangers started coming to our exercise site at Purple Bamboo Park. They stood nearby wearing dark sunglasses and watched us doing the exercises from start to finish.

An older practitioner, one of the coordinators of the site, once asked them whether they would like to learn, but they shook their heads and continued to stand there.

One day it started to rain during the exercises. We continued to the end as usual—and the strangers did, too.

Later on, many relatives and friends called Dongwei and me to tell us, "We have heard from inside sources that the government is going to suppress Falun Gong. Please take care of yourselves!"

I laughed at this. "Suppress? What do they mean by suppress? Is Uncle Policeman going to arrest us? That is so funny!"

When I was a child, I was always getting lost and asking "Uncle Policeman" for directions. "Uncle" is a term of politeness based on the relative ages of the people involved, as are "Sister," "Grandma," and so on. Out of habit, I continued to use the term "Uncle" even when I met a policeman who was younger than me.

This habit would change after policemen struck my head with a stick and stomped on my face with boots.

———•———

A month after the "4/25 incident," our work unit passed around a document from the central government. It was a statement from the Appeals Bureau of the Central Government and the State Council, after some Falun Gong practitioners had gone to appeal. It stated:

> *Recently, some Falun Gong practitioners have started to spread gossip such as, 'The Public Security Department will soon suppress the practitioners,' or 'Members of the CCP will be dismissed if they continue the practice,' etc. All of these are deceptive rumors. Our Party and the government's attitude is very clear as to the normal practice of the exercises. Now I herewith repeat it again: All the normal activities related to body-health exercises and practices have never been prohibited by the government. Everybody has the freedom to either believe and to practice a certain exercise, or not to believe or practice it.*

After reading that, I turned to my colleagues. "See? You guys worry too much!"

They didn't seem convinced, however, and still suggested I be cautious.

I had a friend who worked at the Central Government agencies. He sniffed at my opinion and said, "Thank God you have been living in Beijing for so many years. You don't even have a sense of political movements. Can't you smell the meaning behind this?!"

"Huh!" I said. "Of course I can't smell it. I'm not a puppy."

But in my heart I wondered, *Am I really too naïve?*

Still, I doubt even they could have anticipated the events to come.

———•———

It was a scorching, suffocating July in 1999, as if the gods themselves were incensed by the events that were unfolding.

I ate lots of ice cream to try to stay cool. When Dongwei, who is six inches taller than me, saw me eating, he would say, "Little girl, try harder. I don't think you'll grow as tall as me, but if you really work at it, you might be able to reach the same weight as me!"

In mid-July, for some reason unknown to me, almost all foreign websites became inaccessible. I suddenly couldn't get any information at all outside my immediate circle.

On the morning of July 21, a girl from our study group called me and told me she was able to break through the Internet blockade. She had learned that the day before, the Public Security Department had begun a nationwide arrest of practitioners. They arrested all practitioners they thought were "key" members of Falun Gong.

Only later did I find out that many people had already been arrested just after the April 25 incident, including the members of the Falun Dafa Research Association.

My brain went blank. Practitioners being arrested?! Could this really happen? Mass arrests are not supposed to happen in real life—but it was happening. What's more, it was happening to us—to Falun Gong, such a peaceful cultivation group!

I had a vague premonition that I was not living in an ordinary time, but in a unique one with boundless variables and mysteries hidden within it, and that many things that might happen in the near future were far beyond my imagination.

The girl who called told me that a lot of people were preparing to go to Zhongnanhai again to appeal, and asked if we wanted to join them.

For a split second, I was bound by fear, partly because I didn't know what I would have to face, and partly because I was complacent in the current peaceful, cozy, and blissful time.

I hesitated and didn't know what to do.

The girl was a university student who had just graduated and was several years younger than I. She was also in a bit of a panic, and was seeking advice about whether we should go or not.

I thought for a while and said, "It's not right to detain practitioners. We can't just sit by without doing anything. Let's go and see."

After hanging up the phone, I briefly described the situation to Dongwei. He was shocked as well. We were both perplexed, but we decided to go because someone needed to express the real situation to the government.

Shortly after eight in the morning, our taxi stopped on Fuyou Street near Zhongnanhai. The driver told us that the road was already blocked and that martial law had been enforced. We got out of the taxi and were planning to walk to Zhongnanhai, but we noticed many people who were walking toward us.

Seeing their peaceful, solemn expressions, I guessed that they must also be Falun Gong practitioners who had come to appeal. We asked a young man who walked by us, "Why are you walking this way? Isn't Zhongnanhai over there?"

He replied, "All the practitioners who went to appeal near Zhongnanhai were taken away in police vans. We're going to try the Appeals Office."

We realized we were standing on the other side of the Appeals Office.

More and more practitioners started to gather, just like on "4/25," and stood on the sidewalk in four or five rows, leaving enough walking room for pedestrians. But the feeling was completely different from last time. The atmosphere was tense, stunned.

I took a look at the people around me. There were boys and girls—middle school students, and old men and women with white hair and resolute expressions. Also many middle-aged and young people, some of whom used their cell phones to call their workplaces and ask for a vacation day.

There was a young mother carrying an infant. We moved out of the way so she could stand in the shade.

Seeing all these people, I could not hold back my tears. Every one of us was a member of society, with a job and family, and we were only trying to be better people through cultivation. Could this society not even tolerate people who try to be kind? Why were they doing this to us?

A few more people joined the line. They had tanned skin and a hint of weariness, and I decided that they must be laborers. One of them told us they were from a county in Hebei Province. In order to escape being abducted by the Public Security Bureau, they had hidden in cornfields all night, finally sneaking away at dawn and walking to Beijing.

Some practitioners around us silently passed bottles of water to them in a gesture of respect.

The morning was still warm from the previous day and turned ever warmer as the sun rose higher. Sweat drenched our clothes.

By 10 a.m., more than five thousand people had gathered around the Appeals office. Everyone was anxious, but we stood outside in a disciplined fashion, waiting for someone to receive us.

Word came from the front that workers from the Appeals Office had emerged and wanted to see an appeals letter. A few written statements were quickly passed over to them. Our hearts were moved, hoping the problem could be resolved.

Time passed, but there was no news from the Appeals Office. All of a sudden, dozens of army trucks arrived, and we were surrounded by almost a thousand armed policemen. The road was barricaded and no one could get in or out. Dozens of big buses pulled up, presumably to transport us away.

Practitioners nudged closer to each other. Someone said, "Let's join arms and not go on the bus!" And so we grabbed each other. On my right side was a middle-aged farmer from another province who had dark, dirty arms. I hesitated for a moment before taking his arm and then felt bad for having hesitated.

The armed police lined up in front of us and did a few stunts under the leader's command. Since my childhood, I had spent most of my time at home, school or work. All my life, I'd seen only "refined" people who "fought with their mouths and not their fists." Even in terms of policemen, I'd only seen traffic police.

This was the first time I saw armed police "performing" in real life. I was a little afraid. Nevertheless, there was a thought that encouraged me deep in my heart—we have done nothing wrong. Truthfulness, Compassion, and Tolerance will never be wrong.

We began reciting the introduction to *Zhuan Falun*, which most of us had memorized. The pure words surrounded us. A wide-eyed policeman stared, listening attentively. This was probably the first time he had participated in such a task, and he didn't know what he was facing.

Suddenly, a man carrying a camera came by, taking pictures of everyone. Then several armed policemen came and tried to pull practitioners away by force.

We chanted in unison, "Respect the Constitution, you're not allowed to abduct people! Respect the Constitution, you're not allowed to abduct people!" These sincere words from the bottom of our hearts touched everyone present. Whether it was because of the injustice or because I was so touched, tears suddenly began to roll down my face, and everything was blurred.

The policemen stepped back.

Then came a few men dressed in Lieutenant General military uniforms. They gathered together as if to discuss something. Then at around 11:30 a.m., the police began trying to take practitioners by force again.

They rushed into our line, pushing us apart, cutting us off, and surrounding each divided segment of practitioners. Pulling and dragging, they forced practitioners into the police vans.

Some refused to get in, and others jumped down again after being pulled up. The police rushed over and beat them.

I saw several policemen beating a 30-year-old male practitioner, using their boots to kick his stomach violently. He bent over with each kick, rolling on the ground in pain.

When they came to our group, they did the same thing. A group of policemen rushed up. A slightly plump, middle-aged policeman came toward me. He hesitated a moment and stopped in front of me. "Get on the van yourself."

I knew that I couldn't resist physically and began walking toward a van. A few steps later, a well-built young policeman rushed toward me, madly shouting, "So you finally decided to get on the van? What were you doing just now?"

As he shouted, he raised his fist to throw a punch at me. I was shocked to see his fist aimed at me, and my legs froze. Just as his fist was about to reach my face, Dongwei and another male practitioner raised their arms in front of me simultaneously and took the blow for me.

Then I was brutally pushed into the van. Practitioners were being stuffed into the van until there was no more space. They shut the door and drove away.

In fact, there were many more practitioners than police that day. But Teacher Li taught us that as a practitioner, one should not fight back when being punched or insulted. Not a single person retaliated. Every practitioner withstood the beatings in silence.

We gave up our seats to elderly practitioners and adjusted our postures to help other people gain more space. I was suddenly reminded of that young mother with her little baby. What could have happened to her? Would the policemen throw her into the van too?

Perhaps the driver lost his way, or perhaps he was trying to avoid crowded streets, but the bus took more than two hours to reach Shijingshan Stadium. There were already tens of thousands of people there. Many practitioners were sitting on the floor, silently reciting Falun Gong teachings.

Later on, the work units of employed practitioners came and collected their employees. From that day on, every Falun Gong practitioner, including me and Dongwei, was monitored, restricted, and deprived of their rights at work.

Also from that day on, Falun Gong practitioners nationwide began a peaceful and arduous effort to resist the persecution, using all forms and methods to expose the facts of the persecution to people who believed the CCP's lies and propaganda.

CHAPTER FIVE

July 1999 was an unforgettable month for Falun Gong practitioners. Everything that happened dealt great blows to our heart and spirit, and it was the greatest tribulation and test in our cultivation path thus far.

Around 3 p.m. on July 22, I was at work when the company summoned everyone in all the departments to put down their work, no matter how important it might be, and attend a meeting in the conference room immediately. Everyone sensed something was up and began discussing with each other.

Since it had only been the day before that I had gone to appeal against the nationwide arrests, I thought it probably had something to do with Falun Gong, but I had no idea what.

The director entered the conference room and said a few words about the importance of the matter. Then he switched on the TV.

The television started broadcasting a series of bloody pictures. It was anti-Falun Gong propaganda, supposedly showing Falun Gong disciples who had committed suicide, and a myriad of other things vilifying Falun Gong, including people who had supposedly cut open their abdomens to "find the Falun."

I was dumbstruck. The frightening background music and narration made it even worse.

I was stunned for a long time. The first thing I did after I regained my senses was to look at the channel logo—CCTV 1, for

China Central Television. It was clear and unmistakable. Everyone in mainland China knows that CCTV 1 is the mouthpiece of the Party. Whatever it broadcasts is the same as Party documents. Even then, I could not believe it. How could such "news" be broadcast from an official state media source?

Anyone could see that the content was beyond absurd, but I was concerned about such horrific images being broadcast in such a vivid manner. Wouldn't it frighten any children who might see it?

Later I found out they didn't deem these programs unsuitable for children at all. On the contrary, kindergartens across the nation were forced to broadcast the images to their students. I couldn't bear to think about the countless innocent children across the nation being forced to watch such horrible, explicit images.

After watching this, everyone at work was forced to declare their agreement with the Party's stance. Instead of having me join the large group, however, I was asked to attend a one-on-one interview.

During the interview, the propaganda on the television was not mentioned. Instead, they told me, "You know full well what's going on here. A young, educated person like you ought to be wise. As long as you recognize that you've been cheated, and turn back right now, you will not be affected in any way."

I was a senior worker in my unit. My superiors had always treated me well, and I normally felt quite relaxed with them. However, when they spoke to me that day, I felt an immense weight pressing on me.

I regained my composure and sincerely told them, "Even though I'm young, I've been through years of hardship looking for the true meaning of life. Even though I've had a good life, my spiritual worries were unbearable. That changed the day I read *Zhuan Falun*. I cannot describe how deeply I was touched by it. It resolved all the problems in my heart. From life, the universe, to everything I know, it helped me regain the path to return to my true self, deep inside me. So there is no one cheating me at all. There is no concept of being cheated here."

My superior appeared to be touched by what I said about the meaning of life. He paused for a while and said, "I know that you definitely think it's good—that's why you study it. But are you completely sure this organization doesn't have other goals or ambitions?"

I replied, "Everyone in it is just like me. We're all here to cultivate. What kind of goals would we have? Just a month ago, you held a meeting in which you discussed the Party's documents on the rights of people to believe or not believe in anything they want. What is happening now? I'm confused!"

He seemed embarrassed for a moment and didn't reply.

I continued, "Do you think there are any negative influences that I've brought to the company or my colleagues since I started practicing Falun Gong? Didn't I improve and become a better employee?"

My superior was probably reminded of my excellent performance and decided that he did not want to continue the conversation. He said, "Regardless, the government has ruled that no one is allowed to practice Falun Gong. You're a member of society, and you have to obey national laws, don't you?"

I asked, "By not practicing, do you mean we are not allowed to believe in or adhere to the principles of Truthfulness, Compassion, and Tolerance?"

My superior was a rational man. He knew it was impossible to monitor one's mind, so he brought up several concrete requirements, from not participating in Falun Gong activities to not discussing the issue with colleagues. He was now finished with his job, and he stopped listening to me.

On the way home from work, every television in restaurants, malls, and shops was broadcasting the explicit images. Voices of hate echoed throughout the 9.6 million square kilometers of China. To many, it was as if another Cultural Revolution had dawned.

When I returned home, Dongwei's expression told me that he was feeling the same as I was. We quickly made some dinner and sat down in silence. In the past, we would often watch a little television during dinner, but now every time my eyes fell on the TV, my mind began replaying those frightening images. The black TV stood on the table like a monster. I was afraid it might start shouting and broadcasting the bloody pictures again at any moment.

The broadcast was worse than any horror movie I'd ever seen. Normally, horror movies have a story line where one can at least know what to expect. But here, there was no logic or story line. We had no idea what would come next.

After dinner, we sat on the sofa. Finally I could let down my guard after a day of putting up a strong front. I curled up in Dongwei's arms and tears flowed down my cheeks. "Why? Why?" I said.

Dongwei patted my back. "I don't know why. It's not in the book of *Ten Thousand Whys*."

In the days that followed, the television, radio, and every possible media outlet continued to repeat the same content. All major newspapers carried one story after another, using lie-filled propaganda to launch an all-out criminalization of Falun Gong.

My colleagues began discussing the issue, sometimes openly, other times secretly. Some backed away when they saw me, as if they were afraid I might do some horrible bloody thing right there in the office.

Later, a colleague, referring to the lie that 1,400 people had died from practicing Falun Gong, asked me, "I know that as Falun Gong practitioners, killing is strictly prohibited, but could those 1,400 cases be fake?"

"I have no way of investigating," I said, "but we can look at it logically. Falun Gong has been practiced for seven years, and you know there are so many practitioners in the parks every morning. If we were really like what the television says, what would society look like? Have you heard of anything like this before today?"

He shook his head. "No, I haven't. But in any case, your safety is most important. You have to be careful."

Sometimes colleagues would ask, "I know that you are all good people, but are you sure that your Teacher did not amass a bunch of money somewhere?"

I would reply, "I've been learning Falun Gong for years. The only money I spent was to buy the books. Everything else was free. But let me ask you, aren't most bestselling authors rich? Even if our Teacher is rich, there's nothing wrong with that; it's a market norm. Besides, since 1996, the books have been banned, and the only books printed were all pirated copies. So our Teacher didn't have a source of income from us at all after that."

Some would say, "Truthfulness, Compassion, and Tolerance is good, that's true. But there are many descriptions in Falun Gong teachings about Buddhas, Taos, and gods. That's all superstition, of course—it doesn't agree with scientific principles."

I'd reply, "Traditional Chinese culture is deeply rooted in Buddhist and Taoist culture. It was only in the past few decades that people stopped believing in God. I would expect Falun Gong to be verifiable by science, but even if we can't prove something scientifically yet, it could still be true. It's to be expected that modern science doesn't know everything yet. For example, could you solve differential equations using elementary school mathematics? Our current science is not as far advanced as we'd like to think. There are obviously a lot of things we don't understand yet—wouldn't you agree?"

I was trying to explain the practice to them using logic, but this violent turn of events had hit me hard. I had really never cared at all about the Party one way or the other. It was too far from my sense of reality, from what I had ever wanted in my life.

During lessons on politics in school, I would secretly read a romance novel. Before cultivation, I longed for a romantic, artistic love life. After learning Falun Gong, I longed for a peaceful, tranquil life of cultivation.

After growing up, I had a certain understanding of the brainwashing style of education I'd received in China since I was young, and I could see through many of the CCP's lies. For example, it was said that "without the CCP, there would be no new China." But other countries without communism were doing just fine.

Because I was still young when the Cultural Revolution ended and had received my education from the Party, I was not aware of the atrocities it had committed during its periodic persecutions and purges. I assumed the CCP was an ordinary government, and I thought we lived in a civilized society. I couldn't understand it when people became worried and uptight about the CCP. I thought, *How bad can it be?*

But now, faced with this overpowering political propaganda, I felt the greatest pressure I'd ever felt in my life. Every day, I saw and heard denigrating lies about the things I held most dear. Pressure permeated every aspect of my life, my work, and my environment. Even the air was suffocating, and I often found it hard just to breathe.

During that time, the capital city experienced its highest temperatures in the past century, averaging over 45 degrees Celsius (115 degrees Fahrenheit) for many days.

Yet Dongwei and I did not feel hot or cold, hungry or full. Our inner torture numbed us from the external environment. Every night we sat silent after dinner, not knowing what to do.

But one thing was absolutely clear. Inside, both of us knew— Falun Gong was being treated unjustly. Believing in Truthfulness, Compassion, and Tolerance would never be wrong.

———◆———

Since I was young, I have been an emotional person, but I never cried very much. Even if I was filled with unhappiness, I seldom let it overcome me, so I never shed tears.

I remember once I read a report that said girls who cry a lot live longer because it helps eliminate a toxic substance that is released through tears. I thought that I should perhaps find a good reason to cry once in a while to get rid of this toxic substance.

But after meeting Dongwei, it was difficult to find such a reason. He was always great at cheering me up, and shedding tears became a distant thought.

I'm more outgoing and he is more introverted, which caused some people to think I was bossing him around. But in fact, his mind is much quicker than mine.

When we were together, he would often tease me. He might say, "You have pretty good foresight," and then as the compliment went to my head, he would add, "It looks like the partner you found is much better than the one I found."

In the past, one of his favorite jokes when introducing me was to say, "This is Hongwei, my ex-girlfriend."

"Well, what about now?" people would ask, puzzled.

"Now? She's my wife!"

After July 1999, our normal way of being was disrupted. Dongwei lost his smile, and I began to cry all the time because living was now a tragedy. An empty void replaced our previous joy.

Our plans for a baby also came to a halt. All we wanted was to clear Falun Gong's name and redress the injustice. Having a child didn't make sense at that point.

After the persecution began, almost all overseas websites suddenly became inaccessible. In this information vacuum, Chinese citizens had no alternative to the brainwashing poured out by state media.

Under such overwhelming propaganda, doubts would sometimes flash across my mind. Is Falun Gong really what they say it is? But once I opened up *Zhuan Falun* and read a single sentence, such doubts would immediately be extinguished. Who could possibly fabricate such profound principles?

After the Party destroyed millions of Falun Gong books, many Chinese people didn't know much about Falun Gong. Since it had already been banned, they didn't feel there was much reason to explore the subject. Thus, they had little opportunity to learn that the state-led persecution was based on lies.

Months later, a friend sent me some break-through software that allowed me to access foreign websites. It was then that I found out that Falun Gong practitioners from across the country were traveling to Beijing to appeal to the government.

For months, more than 700,000 people were constantly gathered around Beijing to appeal to the government on behalf of Falun Gong. These people were scholars, students, soldiers, government officials, businessmen, young children, and elderly people.

Everyone came with the singular pure heart to tell the government, the Chinese people, and the entire world that "Falun Gong is Good!"

There were even farmers from faraway provinces like Sichuan, Yunnan, Heilongjiang, Xinjiang, and villagers who had never set foot out of their villages their entire lives. Now they traveled thousands of miles across the nation to speak up for truth.

There was a woman from Baishan City, Jilin Province. On her bus trip to Beijing, she was intercepted by policemen in Liaoning, who confiscated all her possessions. She managed to escape from the police station and walked to Beijing in the bitter cold, begging for food along the way.

A farmer was stopped in Tiananmen Square by the police, who asked what was in his parcel. He opened the parcel to reveal nine pairs of worn out shoes. "I've walked all the way from Sichuan to Beijing just to say from the depths of my heart that Falun Gong is Good! The persecution is wrong!"

As I see it, the injustice heaped on Falun Gong is higher than the mountains, deeper than the seas and wider than the skies. There is just no way to describe it.

In Chinese history, one of the most well-known stories of injustice is that of Dou E, a young widow who was wrongly accused of murdering someone. I thought about Dou E's story, and I couldn't help but compare it to the injustice toward Falun Dafa practitioners. The offense is magnified infinitely, as the practice is infinitely good. Poor Dou E's plight pales in comparison.

As a result, every time I told others about the injustice against Falun Gong, I would become emotional and cry easily.

One day, I met a former Falun Dafa practitioner from the same practice site, Purple Bamboo Park. We chatted a bit as we were walking in the same direction, and I learned something from him about how the faked reports on television about Falun Gong came to be.

He was in his forties and had suffered an accident at work several years before learning Falun Gong. The accident had broken his back, and he had lain in bed, paralyzed, until someone introduced him to Falun Gong. The practice had healed him, and now he could walk again. He regained vigorous health.

His workplace thus saved a huge amount on medical expenses after he began cultivating, and his boss supported him in his practice. His company even invited him to introduce the practice to others in the workplace, hoping to further reduce medical expenses.

After July 20, a few men from CCTV and the Beijing television station showed up one day at his workplace. They took him aside and asked him to slander Falun Gong on TV. They told him to say that after practicing Falun Gong, he had become paralyzed, and he only recovered after he stopped the practice.

Of course his workplace knew what had really happened, but they also pressured him to agree to do it.

He refused. He was then told by the workplace's security office, the Protection Section, "You really have to do what they tell you. If you don't, we'll break your leg and you'll be crawling out of here."

He wasn't about to do such a thing, nor did he wish to have his leg broken. In the end, he somehow escaped and hid in another city for a month.

When he returned, he heard that the workplace leader had been punished by the authorities for being unable to force his employee to slander Falun Gong, but the television station did not return.

Before hearing his story, I already knew that the propaganda was all fabricated. Nevertheless, I was shocked to hear what had happened to him. It was unimaginable to me that anyone would use such underhanded means.

After that, Dongwei and I realized we couldn't remain silent anymore, so we decided to write an appeal letter to the Party leaders. We figured the Party leaders must not know about these things, and that they would definitely intervene if they knew.

Actually, we found out later that many top leaders already knew the true situation of Falun Gong, including that it was good. Many of them even practiced it themselves. In fact, the entire persecution had been initiated by the head of state at the time, Jiang Zemin, against the wishes of many other top leaders in China.

In another incident, a fellow practitioner from Purple Bamboo Park, Ms. Zhao Xin, a lecturer from the Beijing Industry and Commerce University, was arrested by policemen on June 19, 2000, while practicing the exercises at the park.

She was taken to Haidian Detention Center on June 22, and policemen beat her until her neck bone was severely ruptured. She was still handcuffed as she was sent to Haidian Hospital. There she had an operation, after which her entire body became paralyzed. She suffered in pain for six more months before passing away. She was 32 years old.

We didn't know Zhao Xin personally because there were many practitioners at Purple Bamboo Park, but we felt she was one of us. How many more tragedies would take place before things would be resolved?

We began writing letters to all the government leaders and related departments, such as the Public Security Bureau, Judicial Bureau and the People's Courts, to tell them the truth about Falun Gong.

I would often write how Falun Gong helped enlighten me on the meaning of human life, and how it helped me to become a better person. Dongwei explained from a scientific standpoint how Falun Gong is a profound science and is not superstition.

As we wrote the letters, I would often burst into tears suddenly and not be able to continue. My chest was in pain and I felt like my heart was bleeding.

Still, filled with hope, we sent the letters off.

What followed would rip through our lives like a lightning bolt.

CHAPTER SIX

On July 26, 2000, more than a month after we had sent out our signed appeal letters to government leaders and departments, we received our first response.

It was a normal busy work day. I thought about calling Dongwei to ask what he'd like to eat for dinner. Since I worked closer to our home and would get there sooner, I could get dinner started.

I was the chief of my division, so the phone for our office was on my desk. Around three in the afternoon, it rang.

I picked it up. "Hello?"

It was one of Dongwei's colleagues. She delivered the message quickly, as if she didn't know how to break the news to me. "A gang of policemen took Dongwei away at noon. His entire office was ransacked."

"Why?" I blurted, shocked.

At that time, the persecution had been going on for a year, and we had heard many accounts of Falun Gong practitioners being abducted.

"I heard that he wrote some kind of appeal letters to the government."

"He was taken away at noon? Why did you wait until now to call me?"

"We've never had anything like this happen before. We didn't know what to do. We thought you would have both been taken away, and I only just now remembered to call you to make sure."

I thanked her and was preparing to hang up when she said, "I heard that your house telephone has been tapped. Please be careful!"

Indeed, from that day on, our family phone was never safe. Even years after we were released from the labor camp and had changed our phone number multiple times, policemen from the labor camp could always contact us by phone. Whenever I made a call, a voice in my mind reminded me, *Someone else is listening to this conversation.*

Months ago, as I write this now, I was watching the movie *The Lives of Others*. The film's depiction of how citizens of East Germany lived under terror from state police before the collapse of the Berlin Wall is very similar to the situation of people in China today. After the fall of communism in East Germany, people began to reflect on history. The movie *The Lives of Others* has become popular all over the world, even as Chinese citizens still live in the same kind of nightmarish world dramatized by the film.

After the phone call, I went home. I felt lost. The summer heat scorched around me, but I felt cold. I lay sleepless in bed that night.

I felt horrible, wretched, mixed up. I didn't want to stay alone at home without Dongwei. I wanted to be by his side, whatever he was going through.

Several years later, I realized this type of thinking wasn't right. If all the good people are put in prisons and labor camps, who will be left to fight for them?

That night was unbearably long. Finally dawn came, and I arrived at work. I went directly to the company Party secretary's office. He was a thin, bony man, nearing retirement.

I told him Dongwei had been arrested because he wrote letters to the Party leaders to appeal for injustices committed against Falun Gong.

He seemed shocked and nervous. He began criticizing me non-stop. "How could he write such a letter? If you have any ideas, discuss it with the supervising Party secretaries first!"

"All right, well, I'm telling you about it now. Can you help me pass the message on?"

He was stunned and said, "The Party has made its decision. What's the point of passing anything on?"

"Doesn't the Constitution of the PRC guarantee the right to criticize and offer suggestions to the government and its employees?"

His anxiety increased. "Little Comrade Lou, listen to me. Don't criticize or suggest anything. For your own safety."

I said calmly, "I wrote letters, too. We sent them out together."

Even though the air conditioning was on high, the old gentleman broke out in a sweat. He wiped his forehead. When he spoke, his voice sounded tired. "Don't think too much. Get back to work. You have to believe in the Party, in the Party's organization."

"Are you asking me to believe that the Party will, or will not, arrest me?"

Obviously, he didn't expect this question and was stuck for a moment. He couldn't tell me to believe the Party wouldn't arrest me, because as a senior Party member, he knew conventional logic would not explain what the Party might do. And of course he wasn't going to say, "Yes, the Party is going to arrest you."

In the end, he simply repeated, "Just believe in the Party and the Party's organization."

Emerging from the secretary's office, I greeted a few colleagues before walking to Dongwei's workplace. Along the way, I felt immensely heavy inside, as if a huge rock were sitting on my heart. I had difficulty breathing.

I came to a traffic light. Just when I was crossing the road at a green light, a bicycle suddenly came out of nowhere and knocked me down. I fell hard on my knee. The pain sent me kneeling on the ground. It was excruciating for a while, but I endured. My left knee immediately turned purple with bruises. I slowly got up.

The middle-aged woman who had hit me hovered nearby, standing over her bike, looking at me. I wasn't sure why, but I had no desire to fight with her. I simply looked at her and waved her away. "Go ahead and go!"

She looked at my purple knee and pained expression, and guilt seemed to flash across her face. But she didn't say anything and rode away quickly.

I limped to Dongwei's workplace. Seeing me, the company's senior manager hurried over and said, "Ms. Lou, this incident was completely beyond our expectations. They came here to arrest him through our company's security department. We had no say at all. Why don't you go talk to the security department?"

I went to the Protection Section and found the person responsible for Dongwei's arrest. He gave me a brief account and said, "All I could do was ask them not to handcuff Dongwei in front of the other employees. I asked if they would wait for him to get into the car first."

A picture of Dongwei with his hands tightly cuffed appeared in my mind. I could not hold back any longer and tears flowed down my face.

Seeing me cry, the man suddenly flared up and said, "What are you crying about? If you don't want this to happen, don't do such things again! What did you write that letter for?"

"Is this the necessary result of our letter?" I said.

"Yes!" he replied fiercely. "You're in China, and China is like this!"

I stared at him, shocked. Could this be our own doing? Didn't we deserve any sympathy? I wanted to retort, "Dongwei worked at this company tirelessly for five years, and this is how you treat him?"

However, our Teacher taught us that cultivators shouldn't get angry. I bore it inside, but stared at his eyes, trying to decipher what, exactly, he was thinking.

His stare was strangely familiar. An image flashed across my mind and I suddenly remembered—he looked just like the woman who had knocked me down with her bike.

It was a provocative look with a tinge of guilt which seemed to say, "A kind, honest worker was abducted simply because he wrote an appeal letter, and I could not do anything to stop it. I even have to agree with them superficially, for my own safety! It's not my fault—it's because of the communist regime!"

Thinking the situation over, I did not blame him anymore, nor did I know what he could do for us. I stood up and thanked him for requesting that Dongwei not be handcuffed in front of his colleagues. He walked me down the stairs silently.

That night, I braced myself for the same treatment Dongwei had received. I packed everything at home, gave the flowers a good watering, and even found a loose T-shirt. I was prepared to wear it in jail should I be arrested too.

After everything was packed, I opened up my book and looked at Teacher Li's picture. In my heart, I told him, "Teacher, even though I have not had any hardships for the past 30 years, even though this storm came so suddenly, I am not afraid, because you are with me, because Truthfulness, Compassion, and Tolerance is with me."

Seeing Master Li's compassionate smile, strength rose gradually in my heart. I was no longer a weak, helpless girl. I was going to face them bravely.

The next morning, half an hour after I arrived in my office, I was notified to go to the Protection Section.

When I arrived, the room was packed with policemen. I was not surprised.

After they confirmed my identity, I was escorted to a police car. My colleagues stared at me anxiously as they watched me being taken away, but no one said anything.

In the jeep, two policewomen sat at my sides, sandwiching me between them. They brought out a pair of cold handcuffs and shackled me tightly.

From start to finish, I did not say a word. A solemn but stirring sense of courage rose in me. I only had one thought: No matter what lies ahead, I will never falter or retreat, because there is nothing wrong with Truthfulness, Compassion, and Tolerance.

———◆———

As I was taken from my workplace and placed in the police car, I suddenly felt isolated from the external world. The back of the car was sealed, and I had no idea where I was going.

I didn't know how far the jeep traveled, but finally it stopped. When I got out, the first thing I saw was a metal gate flanked by two rows of armed police. The sign beside the gate read, "Beijing City Detention Center."

I was taken to an interrogation room, and my arms and legs were locked onto a chair so I was unable to move. The first question the interrogator asked me was, "Do you know where you are?"

I shook my head.

He raised his voice. "This is the Seventh Division!" Then he studied my expression.

That didn't mean anything to me. "The Seventh Division?" I said. "What's the difference from the Eighth and Ninth Divisions?"

He was surprised I'd never heard of the infamy of the Seventh Division. That left him tongue-tied for a moment.

He could only explain the history of the Seventh Division to me. The Beijing City Detention Center belongs to the Seventh Division (the Major Crimes Division) of the Beijing Public Security Bureau. It was known, at least in name, as the top detention center in the entire country. Every other detention center had regional names, for example the "Haidian District Detention Center of Beijing," or the "Xicheng District Detention Center of Beijing."

Normally, only major criminals who were to get the death penalty or life imprisonment were detained at the Seventh Division.

The floor plan of the Seventh Division is in the shape of a "K." Everyone who's been there knows that once you enter the K building, your priority is to try to stay alive.

Many criminals suffer a psychological collapse when they hear that they've been taken to the Seventh Division, and admit to every crime they've committed. Likewise, the interrogator expected I'd be terrified.

However, I was not affected, because I felt that, as a Falun Gong cultivator, I had lived my life righteously. I had done nothing wrong, and there was nothing to be afraid of. I did not fully fathom the extent of the Communist Party's evilness.

As the saying in China goes, "calves are not afraid of tigers." A calf is too young and naïve to know any better. It didn't occur to me that a truthfully written appeal letter would present any problem. I also assumed my captors would follow the law.

The interrogator continued. "You are still young. Your salary is several times higher than mine, and your house is nicer, too. Why are you against the government?"

I replied sincerely, "On the contrary, I'm not at all against the government. Writing letters actually shows my trust in the government."

He looked at me in disdain. "Do you think the government knows any less than you do? Does the government need your help to tell it what the true situation is? Aren't you just creating trouble?"

I was surprised by this. "If the government is never wrong, why does the Constitution of the PRC guarantee the right for all citizens to criticize and give suggestions to the government and its departments? Otherwise, what's the use of the Appeals Code or the Appeals Office?"

Seeing that I was unafraid, and even answering him logically, he said, "Let's see how tough you are! Wait till you are sentenced to ten years in prison—we'll see how you feel then!"

I was even more surprised. "It is the duty of the People's Court to bring people to trial. Do you have a say in that? Besides, I haven't violated any laws, so how can you treat me like a criminal?"

"You mentioned retribution in your letter. Isn't that publicly threatening government officials? We'll try you and sentence you for making threats!"

I almost laughed at that, but kept my composure. "I didn't make a threat," I said. "Good deeds are rewarded and evil receives retribution. This principle has been around since the birth of Chinese history. Such a statement would only be a blessing for good people. But perhaps evil people would feel that it is a threat."

He shook his head. "You don't sound like you grew up in China— you don't know anything." Suddenly he shouted sternly, "Do you know that the nature of Falun Gong has changed?"

"Falun Gong will forever be Truthfulness, Compassion, and Tolerance."

"Do you know what happened at Tiananmen Square on July 20?"

Actually I didn't. Dongwei and I had been dispatched to Shenzhen and Shandong on work errands before and after July 20, 2000, so we had no idea what happened. Later we learned that my workplace had intentionally sent us out of town to avoid this "sensitive" date.

"Our nation has been in an information blockade. How can anyone know what's going on?"

He shouted at me fiercely, "Falun Gong launched an armed revolt on Tiananmen Square!"

I was stunned, and replied immediately, "That's impossible. We've always followed the principles our Teacher taught. 'As a practitioner, one should not fight back when being punched or insulted.' So how could we possibly mount an armed revolt?!"

"How can the news be fake? It's obvious Falun Gong has its own subversive plans. I think the two of you are too pure. Don't put yourself alongside these people."

I didn't know if he was just trying to create estrangement between me and other Falun Gong practitioners, or if he himself was actually fooled. I could only say, "I do not believe that Falun Gong practitioners would start an armed revolt. If it truly happened, they cannot possibly be Falun Gong practitioners, because such people would be going against the principles of Falun Gong."

The interrogation lasted from morning until night. I was not allowed any food or water. Nevertheless, I remained energetic. The interrogator kept trying to overpower me psychologically, but I simply used the time to clarify what Falun Gong was about. Since the onset of the persecution, who else had taken such a long time to discuss Falun Gong with me?

In the face of truth and reason, he had no grounds to be belligerent.

That night, a policewoman finally escorted me from the interrogation room, past a row of barricades, and into a compound. There were many buildings in the compound, probably full of criminals. At the entrance to one building, she registered me, and we walked in.

The corridor was narrow and dimly lit. The cells at the sides looked like ugly monsters baring their teeth at me. The policewoman opened the door of cell number 513 and motioned for me to go in.

Immediately after I stepped in, the metal gates closed behind me with a *clang* and cut me off from the outside world.

The cell was about 12 square meters in size and barely lit. Just as I was getting my bearings, several people surrounded me. One of them asked, "Are you a Falun Gong practitioner?"

I was stunned for a moment, and replied, "Yes, how did you know?"

A tall girl answered, "We've seen so many people come in and out. There are mostly three types of people sent here: those charged with corruption, those involved in sex scandals—and you don't look like either of those, so you must be the third one—those who're imprisoned for their beliefs."

"Are there other Falun Gong practitioners here?" I glanced around the cell.

She shook her head. "They don't like to group you together unless they really run out of space. There are not many Falun Gong practitioners in Seventh Division, but there seem to be quite a number in the branch bureaus. I've heard that there are a few in every cell."

I was a little disappointed. I had hoped to be able to meet other practitioners and share experiences with each other.

A cultured-looking middle-aged lady asked, "Have you eaten?"
I shook my head.
"I'll get some instant noodles for you," she said.

I felt quite hungry, so I didn't object. A while later, she came over with a bowl in her hands, and pulled me beside her. "Quick, eat!"

I was surprised to find that the noodles were soaked in cold water. She explained that they were only given two tubs of hot water every day, and most of it was used up by noon. As it was the middle of summer, the cold instant noodles tasted good nonetheless.

"Call me Sister Wang," she continued. "Eat this up first. It's almost bedtime—we should go to bed soon. People who've just come in undergo a lot of interrogation. You won't get many chances to sleep."

The pressure of being imprisoned was lightened somewhat by Sister Wang's concern. I said with utmost sincerity, "Thank you very much, Sister Wang."

She paused for a moment. "If you don't mind, you can regard

me as a Falun Gong practitioner, too. I started practicing in prison."

I was thrilled. "Really?! Have you read the book?"

She nodded. "I read it once when I was in the branch bureau's detention center. They don't allow us to bring books in here, they're very strict."

Except for a meter-wide space, the room was filled with wooden boards stacked a foot and a half above the ground, like the rectangular stoves in the northeastern parts of China. There was nothing else in the room.

As a newcomer, I was supposed to sleep on the end closest to the toilet, which they called the "end board," as opposed to the "head board," where the cell leader slept.

Sister Wang wanted to help me beg to be allowed to sleep closer to the inside. I thanked Sister Wang for her kind gesture and told her there was no difference to me. I fell asleep without another thought.

Soon after, I was awakened before dawn. Thanks to Sister's Wang's earlier warning that I would receive many sudden interrogations, I was not alarmed.

Walking out onto the compound, a cold moon hung crookedly in the sky. A few stars blinked lazily. Everything was bleak.

The wind blew against my face, yet I felt like I was in a dream. I felt like I was in a different life.

Have I really been imprisoned? Where is Dongwei right now? When will I see him again?

Two officers began to question me about whether I had been in contact with other Falun Gong practitioners, and who they were.

I finally began to understand why they had arrested me a day after Dongwei. Apparently they thought that after a husband is detained, his wife will feel helpless and contact other Falun Gong practitioners for support. They could follow her and arrest other so-called "organization" members. This could be really dangerous. Fortunately I had not contacted anyone.

Then they began to ask some absurdly detailed questions, such as where I had bought the stamps, where I had printed the letter, and which post office I had gone to.

"I entirely forget," I said. "Don't waste my time asking those kinds of things. I can only tell you honestly that those letters were indeed written by me."

The interrogator could not hold back his laughter. "You want to tell us what we should do? You think we're in your office? We interrogate you because we still pay attention to you. If we left you alone in the cell for a few years, then no one would ever know whether you were dead or alive!"

"Oh, have such things happened here?" I could not help asking. "Is there anyone here you have forgotten, and kept for several years in the Seventh Division?"

They ignored me, so I started thinking maybe it was true. Now I really started worrying about those people. "You need to go check on them—their families will be anxious!"

The officers looked at me with a confused expression. One of them said, "At this time, you can still think of others?" His eyes unexpectedly flashed an unusual mildness.

Because I told them with complete honesty what we had done, explaining the whole story and our experiences of practicing Dafa in detail, after several days of interrogation, there was nothing else for them to ask. One of the interrogators listened earnestly. He actually changed his attitude toward me.

During the final interrogation, the interrogator asked me, "Now that the facts are already clear, at last, I need to know—will you continue to practice?"

I answered without hesitation. "Of course. Why should I not practice something so good?"

His facial expression revealed regret. He sighed and said, "Yep, two bookworms."

From that, I knew Dongwei had told him the same thing.

We were locked up in the Seventh Division for one month. When not being interrogated, we spent the rest of the time in the cell.

CHAPTER SEVEN

Up to that point, our circle of contacts had been defined by education and work—our friends were all basically like us. At the detention center, I met people from other social strata for the first time.

In the Seventh Division, the head of the cell is called the "study leader" or "big sister." Initially, I had heard that the heads of prison cells were all tyrants, burly and rude women who acted like men.

Unexpectedly, our head was a petite and beautiful Sichuan lady. I looked at her and felt admiration in my heart. It was really difficult to imagine her as head of the prison cell.

She had grown up in Chengdu City of Sichuan and moved to Beijing by herself as a young woman. Beijing was a completely different world to her. She ended up with a powerful person as her boyfriend. But he was also the general manager of a huge prostitution ring.

After this was discovered, her boyfriend was charged with being head of the ring. Since she was also involved, she could be sentenced to several years with the charge of "abetting a crime."

She told me, "A while ago, I was in another cell and stayed with one of your fellow practitioners. She is such a good person. No matter how others treat her, she always smiles. She taught me many poems from a Falun Gong book called *Hong Yin*."

She recited one of the poems, "Real Cultivation,"[9] to me:

Cherish Truthfulness, Compassion, Forbearance,
And in Falun Dafa shall you succeed;
Cultivate your xinxing[10] without a moment's pause,
To taste the wonder, so immeasurable, at Consummation.[11]

I suddenly felt close to her.

"I shall treat you well," she said. "But you mustn't practice the exercises."

"I don't think that's good," I said. "I have to think about it, I can't promise you that yet."

Her gentle face suddenly became serious. "You know, your fellow practitioner next door tried practicing, and all the people in her cell were tortured with electric batons. You are all kind people. You can't do such a thing and harm other people."

When she said this, it was hard for me to persist. This was the CCP's sinister method of using the "responsibility system" when suppressing people. A person might be prepared to be steadfast in the face of enormous pressure, but how can one remain resolute when others will suffer, too? Family members and friends are often threatened, making resistance very difficult.

———•———

During this period, the person with whom I had the most contact was the elder Sister Wang. She even worked in the same industry as me, as a branch financial director of a large bank.

One of her friends had told her he had a great investment opportunity and persuaded her to take some money from the bank, promising to return it in several days. So she removed several million yuan from an inactive bank account, thinking he would return the money within a few days and nobody would notice.

It turned out the friend ran away with the money, and Ms. Wang was arrested. After being cheated by her friend, her heart was filled with anger and hatred, and she no longer wanted to believe anything.

After her arrest, she was locked up with an elderly Falun Gong practitioner. That practitioner listened to her encounter and started

9   Li Hongzhi, *Hong Yin*. "Real Cultivation." (English trans. A) December 27, 1994
10   *xinxing* (shin-shing)—mind or heart nature; moral character.
11   "Consummation" refers to enlightenment.

telling her about the contents of *Zhuan Falun*.

Ms. Wang realized she had found a treasure, and her resentfulness slowly diminished. Later, another practitioner was brought in, and she was actually able to bring in *Zhuan Falun*. It was not easy to bring such a book into a cell, but Falun Gong practitioners could sometimes sneak one in. Therefore, Ms. Wang had a chance to read through it once, and she decided to join the practice.

Soon afterward, because her case involved a huge amount of money, she was transferred to the Seventh Division and sentenced to life imprisonment. However, because she had learned Falun Gong, she appeared to be the most peaceful person in the cell.

She told me that no matter where she was, she would always conduct herself according to the standards of Truthfulness, Compassion, and Tolerance in her future life. She desperately hoped that Falun Gong would be redressed soon, so that she could read *Zhuan Falun* again.

After a week, another lady in the cell, Sister Yang, also began to learn Falun Gong from me. Sister Yang was from Guangxi Province and had been arrested for dealing drugs. It was said that her sentence would depend on the amount of drugs that had been confiscated, and she might possibly receive the death penalty or life imprisonment. She had not yet had a trial.

She was hot-tempered, and most of the inmates were somewhat afraid of her. She was only close to me and wanted to learn Falun Gong from me. Sister Yang told me that she had not been a tough person when she was young, but because of her poor family circumstances, she was always bullied, and thus formed this character in order to survive.

She said, "If I had known these principles earlier, I would not be here today."

I spent two weeks recalling to her the main contents of *Zhuan Falun*, and taught her to recite the introduction to *Zhuan Falun* from memory.

One day, the guards ordered everyone in the cell to stand for a whole day. We were being punished but hadn't been told why. Most of the women had bloated legs and feet by the end of the day.

Sister Yang told me that when she was standing there, she recited the introduction several dozen times, and her whole body was light and extremely comfortable.

One morning, Sister Yang woke up crying. Everybody was

surprised to see such a fierce woman burst into tears. She told me that she had finally seen *Zhuan Falun* in a dream.

She asked me through her tears, "Do you think I still have a chance to read it in this lifetime?"

I thought about it. "I don't know. If your heart is sincere, perhaps there will be a chance."

Sister Yang told me once that a young inmate who had been sentenced to life imprisonment for embezzlement secretly told her, "It would be better not to have so much contact with Falun Gong practitioners—after all, they're political offenders."

The CCP has instilled so much deep-seated fear into the minds of the Chinese people, more with each successive political movement, that even prisoners in detention centers, waiting to see if they will live or die, are afraid of being implicated by the CCP for associating with so-called political offenders.

But this didn't affect Sister Yang. She told the woman, "If I am sentenced to death, I'll lose my life. Why would I fear association with political offenders?"

———•———

In detention centers, it is common for newcomers to get cursed at and beaten up by other prisoners. Fortunately for me, the people in my cell had a certain understanding of Falun Gong, and many of them admired Falun Gong practitioners quite a lot, so they took relatively good care of me.

One of the prisoners told me that one time a guard said to her, "If you have a chance to get out of here, don't do any more bad things. Be a moral and noble person like Falun Gong practitioners."

There was another reason they treated me well. Most of the detainees in the Seventh Division were death-row inmates. Many of them had taken someone's life, but many others had received the death penalty without just reason. In China, there is an old saying that the spirit of a person who unjustly suffered a premature death would remain and interfere with the human world. Many prisoners and even some police officers had indeed experienced "seeing ghosts." As a result, people were panic-stricken at night, and some of them had a difficult time falling asleep.

However, since they began putting Falun Gong practitioners in the prisons, the ghosts had gone into hiding. So these prisoners felt that Falun Gong practitioners were unusual—even the ghosts didn't dare to get near them. The prisoners felt secure and were able to sleep at night when a Falun Gong practitioner was there.

———— • ————

In the Seventh Division, the main activity during the daytime was "sitting on a board." Maybe it sounds easy, but sitting for a long time is a painful form of torture. The body must be straight, and the board is hard. After sitting for a long time, one's buttocks and waist become sore and painful.

Once an inmate asked me to help rub her back in the shower. I saw an area on her buttocks that was black and blue. I asked, "How come your backside is blue? Who beat you?"

She answered, "After sitting for several months, you will look like this, too!"

When we had to sit on the board during the daytime, we were not allowed to talk. However, our "head of the cell" was relatively considerate, so when we talked in a low voice, she pretended not to hear anything.

As we sat, I explained to Sister Yang the main contents of *Zhuan Falun*, and when everyone casually chatted, I also explained about the persecution to others.

Sometimes I missed my home and Dongwei. Although we were physically near each other, it seemed as though we were separated by an ocean. We were unable to get any news about each other, and I often wondered how he was doing.

At the Seventh Division of Beijing Police Bureau, my number one priority was to tell Sister Wang and Sister Yang as many of Teacher's lectures as possible. Since I was so focused on trying to recall the lectures, I paid little attention to the food or living conditions.

Thinking back, it seemed that we had the same two meals every day—buns for lunch, a corn bread roll and boiled potatoes for dinner. I can't remember how it tasted, but I can't forget the mud on the potatoes.

Prisoners who had money could order extra food, unreasonably priced, such as instant noodles, milk powder, and sugar.

———— • ————

August 19 was my birthday. The inmates in my cell planned to make a birthday cake for me. I was really curious to see how they might do it in such a strictly controlled environment.

They smashed a corn bread roll saved from the previous dinner, ground it into powder, mixed it with milk powder and sugar, and kneaded the dough. The corn bread became soft, and they let it sit for a while until they felt it was ready.

As I looked at this carefully made cake, I was speechless.

I had eaten many birthday cakes with all kinds of flavors and from well-known bakeries. But I had never had anything quite like this. A corn bread cake at the detention center. It was actually tasty, too. My cellmates were happy to see me enjoying it.

———•———

One day, some guards took Sister Wang out for a long conversation. She did not say anything on her return, but after that, she stayed away from me and never spoke with me again. I knew the guards had threatened her.

Even though she never said anything, she always remained kind to me and did as much as she could for me without saying a word. She mended my quilt cover, sewed buttons for me, and even washed my clothes.

Sewing a quilt cover or button is a simple task in the outside world, but at the detention center it was a major project because we didn't have needles or thread. We did it by taking threads from old clothes. Then we used the tip of a toothbrush to prick a small hole in the cloth, then we poked the thread through. It took a lot of time to sew on a single button.

———•———

Sister Yang was a strong lady and not afraid of anything. She continued to learn from me, reciting *Hong Yin*, poems written by Teacher Li. None of the guards stopped her. Sister Yang recited the poems before sleep, during on-duty time,[12] and even when she was eating. After a month, she could recite 72 poems from *Hong Yin*.

Gradually her pale face started to turn pink, and she climbed out of the shadow of death.

My month at the detention center passed rather quickly. I knew that the maximum duration for criminal detention was one month. After that, a person would either be released or formally arrested, in which case they would begin to go through a legal process.

I felt that the chance of my being formally arrested was slim

---

12 On-duty time was when two inmates stayed up all night to watch the others in case someone tried to commit suicide or kill another inmate.

because it would be a joke if the police wanted to use our letters as "evidence." So I began preparing for my release and giving my things to those who would not be released.

One day, the head of the cell and I were on duty together. Seeing that I was optimistic, she told me to "have one red heart but prepare for two scenarios."

I didn't understand.

She said, "They asked you to write a statement that you wouldn't practice Falun Gong anymore, but you refused to do so. How can they let you go?"

"But sentencing somebody is a legal process," I said. "Why would it have anything to do with whether a person writes a statement?"

Looking at me, she smiled. "Your thinking is so simple. I hope you will reach Consummation through cultivation soon."

The next morning, I was taken for interrogation. The two interrogators were stiff and motionless. They asked, "Are you doing well?"

I answered, "How well can I be, staying in the detention center? You should release me immediately. I did not commit any crime and I should not be kept here."

One interrogator gave me a strange look. He took a sheet of paper out of an envelope and read it loudly. "Hongwei Lou, female, 30 years old, Beijing citizen, is sentenced to one year of forced labor for disturbing the social order."

I was shocked. A year? Forced labor? I hadn't completed my project at work. I hadn't informed my colleagues or friends. How could my aging parents handle this?

After a while, I asked them, "How about my husband, Dongwei?"

He answered, "The same. One year of forced labor."

I shook my head. "You are too cruel! You sentence us to a year just for writing letters?"

They did not answer me but instead asked, "Do you want to request an administrative reconsideration?"

"Definitely. Your sentence has no legal basis."

One of them said, without much energy, "Go back and tell the guard that you want to write something for administrative reconsideration. Ask her to bring you paper and pen."

I was taken back to the cell. All the inmates were enraged after finding out I had been sentenced to a year of forced labor. They also tried to comfort me. "You know, it's the lightest sentencing we've heard for someone coming out of the Seventh Division."

I felt really aggrieved. I had written those appeal letters sincerely and hoped the government could reassess Falun Gong. How could that end with a forced labor sentence?

I couldn't believe the brutality of it. I felt tears in my eyes. Not wanting to let the others see me crying, I went to wash my face.

Before I finished washing, Sister Wang and Sister Yang came in and held me and started crying, too. The tears I had just held back poured out like water from a broken dam. The three of us held each other and cried hard.

We all knew that my leaving might mean a permanent separation for us, and the chance to meet again would be slim. They each stood at one side of me, held my hand tightly and told me, "Young sister, don't worry about us. We will cultivate well and be good people!"

I was delighted by that. Two more people had found the most precious thing. However much I felt wronged, it was worth it.

The inmates in our cell normally did not let us three stay together too long, to avoid trouble from the guards, but that night nobody said anything. We stayed together and recited poems from *Hong Yin* for a long time.

The next morning, I was told to pack for the forced labor camp. I said, "But I want to request administrative reconsideration. How come you've started carrying out the sentence already?"

One guard answered, "You can write the request when you're at the labor camp." Then she mumbled, "Not that it'll do any good."

When I left the building, I saw Dongwei!

His hair was cut very short, quite different from how I remembered his handsome face. He was guarded by a male guard and was to be taken to the forced labor camp with me.

Looking at each other, at first we couldn't speak. Getting closer to me, he asked, "Have you been abused?"

I thought, "Isn't being imprisoned for no reason a big abuse?" But I knew what he meant. He was asking whether I was beaten or harassed by inmates. I shook my head.

He sighed with relief and said, "I was not beaten either. They all respect Falun Gong practitioners. But I heard it's quite bad at the labor camp. Please take care of yourself!"

We were taken to a police car and seated next to each other. My right hand and Dongwei's left were handcuffed together. We held hands tightly with our uncuffed hands, trying to comfort and encourage each other.

Having not seen each other for a month and being imprisoned, we had a lot to say, but it was difficult to say anything. My eyes were blurry with tears.

He tried to tease me to cheer me up. "Well, I can see you managed to lose some weight. You look so slim and attractive." I didn't know whether to laugh or cry.

Our time together passed quickly. The police car stopped at the dispatch center of the forced labor camp in a southern suburb. A policeman and policewoman took us each away.

I realized that we would be separated for a long time. I turned back to see Dongwei. He was looking at me with love and sorrow.

Since we had met, we had looked at each other many times, but I'd never seen this look. The entire dispatch center was quiet for a few seconds, and it was as if nothing around us existed. The only thing was our looking at each other.

Suddenly the policewoman shouted at me, "What are you looking at? Lower your head!" An electric baton pressed my head down until my chin reached my chest.

Then Leo Tolstoy's words came into my head. *Only when you endure the pain of separation can you feel true love.*

But I said to myself, "I am not here to feel true love. Why should we have to endure this man-made separation just for speaking the truth?"

To encourage myself, I began reciting a famous poem by Hungarian poet Sandor Petofi, replacing the word "freedom" with "truth."

Life is dear
Love is dearer
Both can be given up for truth.

CHAPTER EIGHT

On August 29, 2000, Dongwei and I were taken to the dispatch center for detainees at the Beijing Forced Labor Camp. Policewomen took me into the area where they detained female prisoners.

After we were separated, I had to go into a room to register my basic information. There were more than ten new arrivals. After that, we were told to take off all our clothes. I averted my eyes from the others.

During the light of day, we had to stand in an open area, naked. I felt so embarrassed I wanted to find a crack and hide in it.

I did notice a female near me, about my age, whom I later found out was a nurse. What I noticed was that she had long hair with which she could cover a part of her body, and this made me envious. I never thought of hair being used for something like this.

I felt my face flush with embarrassment, and in that moment I thought, "No matter what happens, I'll never have short hair again. Women should have long hair."

We were walked out into the yard with our quilts and were told to sit down on the ground and disassemble them, in order to examine whether there were Falun Gong books or articles hidden or sewn into them. After the policewomen checked the quilts, we were ordered to sew them back together. All of this while naked.

The sun at the end of August is still intense, and glared off our white skin. As we sat there, the heat baked into us.

The female prison area was separated from the outside by just a wire fence. Behind the fence, one could clearly see male policemen walking around. When I was almost in despair and extremely ashamed at having to be naked, a policewoman finally came in with a pile of clothes, saying, "Pick your own size and put it on."

It was uniform clothing, a white short-sleeved shirt and blue shorts. Everyone was in a hurry to get dressed.

After we had put on the clothes, I dared to glance at the other women, who were of various ages.

Next we were told to stand in a line facing the wall. We had to squat down, lower our head, and hold the back of our head in our hands without touching our elbows to our knees. Both our legs and arms quickly became exhausted.

I can't remember how long we had to squat in this position, but if we moved slightly, we were scolded.

After I had endured this almost to my limit, I unexpectedly remembered the detention center, where we sat from morning to night. Although that was very painful, it was not as bad as squatting in this position, thinking I would faint at any moment.

At last, two guard-duty detainees (called "little sentries") came over. They themselves were also prisoners but had been chosen by police officers to monitor other prisoners. They told us to stand up, and they loudly read the prison regulations to us. Then they told each person to loudly repeat, "I am prisoner XXX, …"

Since we had to register before we came here, they knew that the first person in the row was the only non-practitioner. She immediately repeated in a loud voice what they told her to say.

The second person was a female practitioner in her forties, with a dark red complexion. She said, "I did not break the law. I am not a prisoner."

The two "little sentries" appeared to be shocked. They ran toward that practitioner and beat and kicked her. The practitioner fell to the ground but made no sound.

Several police officers sat languidly by and watched the scene. The sounds of the beating didn't disturb them in the slightest.

In the labor camp, police officers didn't personally torture people. They always ordered the guard-duty detainees to do it.

One of the reasons for this is that beating people is really tiring. Another reason is, what if someone died or got a permanent injury from a beating? The police officers could just say they weren't to blame, that it was the inmates who did it.

In order to better execute the beatings, the prisoners chosen to be the little sentries were extremely vicious and menacing. In fact, the female little sentries always looked like men.

I was third in line, and I must admit that I was ignorant from the beginning. I had no idea what to do, but the action of this practitioner helped me to decide that I would definitely not cooperate with them.

Practicing Falun Gong is not wrong. How could I repeat that sentence? And how could I not support the other practitioner who had refused to say it?

The little sentry shouted loudly, "Lou Hongwei, it's your turn!"

I remained quiet, and she was surprised I didn't respond. Maybe she thought that since I was petite, and appeared quite frail, that watching such a violent beating would be sufficient to inspire obedience.

She shouted at me again, "It's your turn! Do you hear me?"

I ignored her and looked straight ahead.

"Do you also want to oppose the government?" she cried out hysterically. "I will say it again, and then I will no longer be polite!"

I knew what to expect, so I tightened my body and got ready for a beating.

But what happened next, I did not expect. She lifted her hand and slapped me in the face with all her strength. Both my ears heard a loud *BANG!* My head felt dizzy and numb, and I felt an unspeakable pain in my jaw.

I had frequently seen scenes in movies or on TV where someone was slapped in the face, and in my mind, it was more shameful than painful. But when she slapped me, I had no time to feel shame because I almost fainted, and the pain in my jaw was beyond imagination.

I know now that she had probably dislocated my jaw, because during the next two weeks, I could hardly open my mouth to eat.

The little sentry noticed the effect her slapping had had, and was satisfied. She shouted, "Read!"

I struggled to stand there, but still did not answer her.

The little sentry stopped for a while and then said to another little sentry, "Take her, and let her 'fly' against the wall!"

"Flying" is a frequent physical torture method used in the labor camps. The person stood me facing a wall and held down my neck, lowering my head until my forehead touched my knees. My face was clamped between my two legs, and then my arms were lifted upward behind me, like wings, until my hands touched the wall.

I had to stay in this position for a while, and I almost lost consciousness. At that time, I really wanted to lose consciousness. I figured at least then I could escape this reality, even if for only a little while.

Behind me was the nurse with the long hair. She also firmly refused to obey but instead explained the situation of the persecution of Falun Gong to the little sentry.

The leader was anxious. "Hey, all you Falun Gong practitioners, it looks like if we are not fierce, you won't be obedient!"

Then she went and talked to several police officers, and they left, probably to get electric batons. The nurse suddenly said in a calm voice, "We Falun Gong practitioners just want to be good people. Why do you threaten us with death like this? I strongly protest!"

After saying this, she ran at full speed and smashed into the wall. I heard a big *THUD*. Even the floor vibrated. The entire dispatch center was silent for several seconds, and then there was chaos as everyone reacted.

I was too shocked to think. I heard a group of people carry her out. I sat down, mourning this practitioner who had sacrificed herself to save us from worse suffering. I began to cry loudly.

A police officer heard me crying and came over. She kicked me flat on the ground and stamped on my head and face with each of her hard leather boots in turn, for about a minute. She said, "Cry, you @%*&#! Cry again, I'll kick you to death!"

My grief and indignation emerged, and I cried even louder. Another police officer came and said to the prison leader, "Quickly take them to the class!"

———◆———

I was allocated to class No. 8, and as soon as I stepped into the room, the people in there asked me with concern, "Who was so strong? We heard it all the way from here!"

Upon hearing that, I recalled the nurse and was concerned about her situation. My tears started flowing again.

One of the women said, "Don't worry—you practitioners are protected by your Teacher, and you won't have a big problem. Look at us. We can't withstand being tortured with electric batons even for a little while, while you Falun Gong practitioners are often fine after being tortured until the batteries are empty, and then being tortured again with new batteries!"

She had meant to comfort me.

"But we still have a mortal body," I said. "How can we withstand being tortured with electric batons?"

"Yes, that's true. An elderly lady was burned last time because she practiced the exercises. But I mean your spirits are strong, and you do not give in. You disregard the torture and recover quickly."

The room we were assigned was long and narrow, with two bunk beds on each side and a corridor in the middle so small that only one person could stand there.

At the entrance, there was a space of one square meter. Wash bowls were placed underneath the beds, and inside the wash bowls were food containers and various things. After everyone sat down on a stool, there was no room for even one more foot.

The person who had just spoken to me was the "class leader," arrested for selling sexual items. She was from Hebei province, about 40 years old, and plump. She was relatively friendly to me. Luckily she was not the scary type.

After this day, I was exhausted. I couldn't imagine staying in that place for a year, and I didn't know if I could survive it.

Before I went to sleep, I said to myself: *This is surely a dream.* When I wake up tomorrow morning, I'll probably be lying in my bed at home. Dongwei will be there next to me, and he'll comfort me, saying, "Don't be afraid. You just had a nightmare. It's gone now, and life is wonderful like before."

But this was only the beginning of the nightmare. When I arrived at the dispatch center, I had only just stepped through the gates of hell.

———— • ————

On the morning of the second day, I was awakened by a rhythmic noise that's difficult to describe. At that moment, I realized that life in the labor camp was not only a nightmare, but also cruel. I began to feel despair from deep within my heart.

I closed my eyes tightly and told myself, "This is only a dream! It is not real! I will wake up in a moment in my own home!"

But the sound of cursing broke my self-deception. When a guard-duty detainee noticed I was still in bed, she rushed into the cell and shouted, "Get up immediately! Are you waiting for my fist?"

Life in the dispatch center cannot be imagined or believed by a person who has not experienced it. Before I was taken there, I would have never believed there could be a place as horrible as this on earth.

The police and the guard-duty detainees looked vicious. They didn't speak, they roared. Their daily routine and disregard for human beings cannot be described in human words.

I often thought I was in a madhouse. But it was worse to be in a dispatch center than to be in a madhouse. This environment was ruled by madness.

Years later, as I recall the dispatch center, the first thing that comes to my mind is the foulness. The foulness was not the fault of the physical environment, but of the intention of those ruling it. We were not allowed to take baths, wash our clothes, or clean when necessary.

Flies covered the sky.

A fly in my home had been a rarity. Whenever Dongwei heard me shout, "Terrible! There's a fly in the house!" he would hurry over and try to remove it for me, so I wouldn't be upset. I couldn't bear the thought of a fly resting on anything in our house. He would practice *Gongfu* to catch the fly in one hand.

In the dispatch center, I really wanted to shout, "Terrible! One, two, three … thousand flies!!!!!"

At mealtimes, when steamed bread in a basket was put on the floor, flies would stick to the bread, forming a black layer. It made me want to vomit.

It was summer. More than ten people were crowded into one small cell. Even if we did nothing, sweat would pour down our bodies like rain. But from six in the morning, from the moment we got up, we were forced to work and not allowed to take a break. Everyone stank.

Morning and evening grooming was limited to two minutes each, including using the toilet.

Our clothes were soaked with sweat several times over each day, and they were quickly covered with a white substance, probably salt from our sweat. If we had taken our clothes off and set them on the ground, they would have stood by themselves.

After surviving torture during the day, we were not at peace for the few hours of sleep at night. The stench from our bodies drew numerous flies to us, crawling all over our faces.

At the beginning, I couldn't bear it, so I tried covering my head with the quilt. But because it was the height of the summer, I felt so hot and dizzy it almost made me faint. When I removed the quilt, the flies were on me again.

Something that still haunts me is that we were not allowed to use the bathroom when we needed to. We were only allowed to go during our two minutes of morning and evening grooming time. We had to speed everything up, or else choose between using the bathroom and washing our face.

Once, when my time was up before I finished brushing my teeth, I decided not to rush out as usual. As a result, the guard-duty detainee hit my neck with a thick wooden stick, driving me out of the bathroom.

At the beginning when I was beaten, I felt angry and humiliated. I felt that I always behaved as an upright person, so why should I be humiliated and insulted like this? No one had ever beaten me. I had been a good daughter from childhood, and my husband also took good care of me. In my home, school, and office, I always associated with well-mannered people who never thought of beating each other.

Yet I was insulted and beaten as soon as I arrived at the dispatch center, and the insults, assaults, and beatings would continue almost every day.

My heart hurt deeply.

After living in that kind of environment for a long time, I became indifferent to being cursed at or beaten. The only thing I cared about was, for example, how I might wash both my face and my feet in one grooming session. I ignored being cursed, and I felt that being beaten was better than the unbearable filth.

Sometimes if I took longer than allowed in the bathroom and was not beaten, I would feel fortunate. In the past I would be unhappy if I heard a heavy word from someone, but now I felt fortunate if I wasn't beaten in the bathroom. Actually, I was suffering from Stockholm syndrome, in which kidnapping victims, over time, get a warped sense of what is normal and develop a measure of sympathy toward their captors. The victim exhibits feelings of gratitude at what is perceived as kindness—which can be simply a lack of abuse in that moment.

Some people had a much harder time with the two-minute rule. There was a woman who needed to sit on the toilet longer than most people, and she wasn't ready when the time was up. She made a request to extend her time for this, but nobody listened to her, and she was unable to relieve herself.

Ten days later, she felt excruciating pain in her abdomen. She was finally allowed to use the bathroom at night after everyone went to bed, but at this point it was not enough, and she was unable to relieve herself.

She went to try again every night. Every morning, others would ask her if she had been successful. It took 20 days before she was finally able to relieve herself. It was said that her stool was full of blood and harder than stone.

One day Sister Ge, who shared the cell with me, got her menstrual period. There were no sanitary napkins in the dispatch center. There was only one roll of toilet paper per day for each cell of ten women, which fell far short of what was needed.

Sister Ge had no choice but to let the blood flow down her legs. Every day, she had to wear the same pair of bloodied trousers. Sometimes the blood could even be seen running down her leg. And the smell of blood drew even more flies into our cell.

The female is the symbol of motherhood. The physical characteristics of the feminine should engender protection and care. I was grieved to see this being turned into an instrument of humiliation and torture.

Seeing such a horrible scene, my body responded instinctively. I didn't get my period for a long time, and this saved me from a lot of humiliation.

————◆————

During the day, we were forced to wrap thousands of pairs of disposable "sanitary" chopsticks. They were delivered in sesame bags to the dispatch center for wrapping.

The bags were opened and the chopsticks dumped in a pile on the ground. We wrapped the tips of the chopsticks (two sticks partially connected) with a thin piece of paper, which was labeled with the printed words "sanitary, feel free to use."

We were not allowed to wash our hands before or after meals or when working. Even after using the toilet, we didn't always have time to wash our hands, and the rationed toilet paper didn't help matters. In such unsanitary conditions, we packed deleterious chopsticks to be sold on the market.

The experience gave me a deeper understanding of the moral deterioration of human beings that our Teacher had talked about. It appeared many people would do anything for money, including give up a clear conscience. Weren't the factory owners and the police concerned that their own friends and relatives might end up using these very chopsticks at a restaurant somewhere?

————— • —————

Something else that sticks in my mind is the phrase "lower the head, hold it on the belly." We were forced to lower our head until our chin touched our chest. We had to lower our head like that whenever the police guard or the detainee guard was talking to us.

I was cursed and beaten many times because my ability to lower my head was not up to their standards. Some people couldn't even hold their head up anymore because they had spent so much time with it lowered. For a long time after I was released, I still automatically lowered my head a lot.

At the dispatch center, I was always on edge because we could suffer physical torture or spiritual humiliation at any moment.

After a while, I was no longer very clear-minded. When in pain, people become like robots. I think maybe it's a kind of self-protection. By becoming numb to the surroundings, one can block out the pain to a certain extent.

Gradually, I became so numb to my surroundings that I no longer realized where I was and no longer even thought about Dongwei.

This really frightened me. If I could no longer even think of the dearest person in my life, had I gone mad?

————— • —————

Falun Gong practitioners detained at the dispatch center were prohibited from speaking to each other. If the policewomen or the more malevolent guard-duty detainees saw practitioners even exchanging looks, the practitioners would be beaten or reprimanded.

But conversations between practitioners and other inmates were not enforced as strictly. So I would often talk to the other inmates I came in contact with about Falun Gong. Initially, the team leader was wary about letting me talk to other inmates, even though practitioners had already told her a lot about *Zhen-Shan-Ren*.

After a while, I helped her write some personal letters to her family. She didn't know how to write many characters, and didn't know what to say to her family. I wrote that she had learned a lot from her roommate and already knew how to be a good person, and that after she returned home, she would try her best to be good in every respect. She would break out in tears when she read the letters I wrote. This was the turning point—after that, she didn't try to stop me from telling people about Falun Gong.

Later, a young girl named Little Ren, who had been convicted of drug addiction, started to practice Falun Gong because of my efforts. The team leader supported her as well. Sometimes, when Little Ren fell back into her old ways, cursing others when she was in a bad mood, or telling a dirty joke, the team leader reminded her, "Now that you've learned Falun Gong, you have to be a good person. Don't go back to your old ways!"

Actually, the team leader would have been glad if everyone learned Falun Gong. This would be of great benefit to her because then her team could be easily supervised and she could take it easy. In fact, all the criminals agreed that if everyone practiced Falun Gong, there would be no need for prisons.

I thought that many more inmates would have learned Falun Gong if it were not for the guard-duty detainees, who were assigned to strictly monitor us.

The meanest guard-duty detainee was a girl surnamed Chang. She was just over 20 years old and serving a sentence for theft. She was a female, but she didn't behave like one. She was darkly tanned and had a heavy build. She was more vicious than some of the men when she beat someone.

Everyone secretly called her "Mad Chang" because she really did seem to be mad. She ran around like a maniac, shouting and screaming all the time. Every time I saw her, I couldn't help shedding tears. I pitied her because no human should behave like that.

Once, for some unknown reason, Mad Chang beat up an elderly, white-haired lady. One could tell at a glance that the gentle old lady was a Falun Gong practitioner. It is unbelievable that anyone that age would be imprisoned in a slave labor camp. It is even forbidden under Chinese law. But with the persecution of Falun Gong, it seemed that laws, morals, and every last strand of humanity had been forsaken.

Chang grabbed the elderly lady's hair with one hand and slapped her several dozen times with the other.

I cried silently because of the suffering of the old lady, but also out of pity for the assailant. These people were raised as atheists, without a single shred of conscience. They had never heard of the universal law of reward and retribution. Sadly, they became the tools of criminals and the totalitarian regime. In this kind of environment, it would never have occurred to her that she might face retribution for doing such terrible things.

One day, Mad Chang approached me, demanding information. "I heard that you've come from the Seventh Division. Do you know Wang XX?"

I was surprised to hear Sister Wang's name. "Yes," I said. "Wang was sentenced to life."

Chang's empty eyes suddenly flickered, and within a few moments tears ran down her face. It was a rare scene indeed. People nearby looked at her curiously.

For perhaps the first time, I heard her say something without shouting. "We shared the same cell. Sister Wang was very kind to me. Such an injustice!"

"Yes, she was kind," I replied. "But she's doing well. She practices Falun Gong now."

"Oh," Chang said, resuming her usual uncaring expression. Then she turned around and barked at the people nearby, "Who said you could listen? Close your eyes!"

I think that because of Sister Wang, Mad Chang never gave me much trouble after that. However, another guard-duty detainee, a 17-year-old girl who had been convicted of sex crimes, always picked on me.

She looked coquettish but appeared somehow abnormal. Every so often she would come to my team and torture me for no reason. Often, just as I had gotten out of bed, she would appear and yell, "You there, go squat by the wall!"

"Why?" I would ask, but she never answered. At the beginning, I just ignored her. Then she dragged me while kicking me with her feet until I was squatting by the wall. I was not afraid of reasoning with her, but she was totally illogical. I didn't know how to handle such physical situations, especially since our Teacher had taught us not to hit back when attacked or insult back when insulted.

Once, my team leader could no longer bear it and asked her, "Do you have something against her? Why are you always torturing her?"

The girl responded, "Look at how snobbish she is. She even wants to be graceful and elegant here! This is a prison! I can't stand people who put up such a front. You'll see how I get her!"

At the time, I treated this incident as a personal grudge. I reminded myself, "Teacher taught us to be considerate of other people everywhere we go. Perhaps it was something I did that provoked her."

Looking carefully within myself, I realized that ever since I was young, I had the notion that people were not worth much if they were not well-educated, and I thought of them as being uncultured. This attitude caused me to look down on those who had not studied.

After I began to cultivate, I realized that this was a bad notion. Cultivators cannot use ordinary people's measures of power, wealth, status, gains, or looks to categorize people. We only have one yardstick: Truthfulness, Compassion, and Tolerance. Those who conform to these principles are good, while those who defy these principles, no matter how powerful or wealthy they might be, we are still to treat with kindness, but they will surely suffer punishment from the heavens.

Later on, I realized that the situation with the girl was not so simple. It was actually a step in their systematic arrangement to "transform"[13] me.

Those who don't understand faith often believe that there are two kinds of people who are the hardest to transform.

First are the uncultured and "stubborn" people, such as elderly ladies or country girls. Many of them were cured of their diseases miraculously, or their family troubles were resolved after they began cultivating. They believe that Falun Gong is without a doubt the best thing one can experience in life. They believe that Teacher is here to save people, and they do not listen to anything anyone else says on the matter.

The second type are highly educated and intelligent people. These people do not believe in anything easily. Their beliefs are based upon serious contemplation, discovery, and their subsequent decisions. Being highly educated, they have a sharp mind, clear logic and reasoning. They are difficult to brainwash. Therefore, the police tactic to transform them is to attack their confidence, make them lose their self-esteem, and finally get them to doubt their own judgment in their faith, leading more easily to "transformation."

I was classified in the second category. They first spiritually humiliated me to make me lose confidence in my own decisions and

---

13 "Transform" is the term the Party uses to refer to its efforts to forcefully convert practitioners away from their belief in Falun Gong. It is common for prisons, labor camps and police stations to receive quotas from the Party for the number of adherents they must convert during a certain time period, a key factor contributing to the large-scale use of torture against practitioners.

judgment. No one discussed anything with me in terms of reason or logic. Some would often humiliate me or torture me for no apparent reason. For instance, after prohibiting me from taking showers or washing my clothes, they would mock me as flies buzzed around me. "See how dirty and smelly Falun Gong practitioners are!" Or, "Look at you, Falun Gong practitioner, you look like a ghost!" especially after cutting and messing up my hair.

They would have me shout words such as, "Reporting! Present! Yes!" hundreds of times, and then mock me. "Look at what happened to these Falun Gong practitioners. They're all insane!"

Throughout Chinese history, the mind has been the symbol of nobility and dignity. The coercive "heads-down" routine at the dispatch center is designed specifically to ruin dignity and tarnish self-esteem.

Perhaps I had lived a simple life in the past. The evil environment at the dispatch center far exceeded my imagination and my limits of tolerance. Slowly, I became muddle-headed and trance-like, and even began to think about death.

In fact, I had always enjoyed my life. My long-term steady relationship with Dongwei made me confident and filled me with gratitude toward life. I used to be quite afraid of death. If I thought of having to die one day, I would become nervous for an extended period. After starting to cultivate, I understood the true meaning of life, and lost my fear of death.

Yet, at the dispatch center, the thought of committing suicide entered my mind for the first time in my life. I often thought, "What's the meaning of a life that's worse than hell?" I had to remind myself that it is a sin for a cultivator to commit suicide. That thought prevented me from going through with it.

One day, I told my team leader, "If they say they are going to execute whoever still practices Falun Gong, I'll be the first one to rush out!" My team leader replied, "Yeah, how easy it is to just get shot by a bullet. They won't let you off that easily. They're going to make your life hell, or worse than hell."

One night, when I had reached the limit of my physical and spiritual endurance, I had a vivid dream. I was strolling around in a library, looking for a book among the shelves. Finally, I found what I wanted. The book was called *Forging Steel*. Teacher's compassionate voice resounded in my ears, "My child, only after countless forgings can true steel be formed."

I woke up, and I instantly felt that my capacity to endure had reached new heights. I had overcome the wish to commit suicide. I told myself, "You are going to walk out of this place alive! You're not as weak as you imagine!"

————•————

The pain one experiences when losing one's freedom cannot be described nor understood by someone who has not experienced it. Being locked up in a small cell, isolated from the rest of the world, one's desire for freedom rises exponentially with the passage of time. When rays of sunlight show through the tiny window, the outside world feels as if it is miles away.

One holds fast to a dream of going for a short walk. When I was at the Seventh Division, everyone from our cell block looked forward to being interrogated because they had to travel to another yard and could see mundane marvels on the way. Despite tall walls and buildings, there were a few trees by the roadside, and we considered them spectacular.

No one would take their eyes off anything along the way, engraving the memory of it in their heart. Those few trees received attention unparalleled in the world beyond the camp. Sometimes it felt as if the trees knew me and waved their branches, even when there was no breeze.

After arriving at the dispatch center, we were rarely able to step outside the prison compound. The only time we could do so was when chopsticks were delivered to the prison. The trucks were parked outside the prison compound, and we had to carry them in, pack after pack.

I can remember the first time a chopstick bag was placed on my shoulder. It weighed dozens of pounds, and my knees immediately buckled, and I collapsed. Even the policewomen could see that I wasn't faking, so I was exempted from the task. But I also lost the chance to catch a glimpse of the outside world.

I had one other chance to leave the prison compound. One day, I was working on a task when a female guard told me that someone from the Education Section wanted to talk to me.

When I stepped through the cell door, two male guards were waiting for me. I was taken from the compound to an air-conditioned office. I was offered a seat opposite them. One guard asked, "How're you doing? Missing your husband?"

"Do you really care?" I asked. "Why not come straight to the point?"

"We still care about you. Both of you are talented people, of great benefit to our nation. We can arrange for you to meet your husband."

What I thought was, "So why did you imprison us in labor camps if our talents are of such great benefit to the nation?"

What I said was, "That'll be good, thanks."

He smiled. "If you write a statement guaranteeing not to practice Falun Gong, we'll arrange it right away."

I wasn't surprised. I knew that they had an ulterior motive for their "kindness."

"If we had wanted to give up our practice just to see each other," I said, "we wouldn't be here in the first place. We could just see each other every day at home—no need to trouble anyone to arrange a meeting."

They appeared rather disappointed and ordered for me to be taken back to my cell immediately.

Before they could usher me out, I asked, "Did you talk to my husband? What did he say?"

"Yes, we approached him first," a different guard replied. "He said he doesn't miss you at all, and he doesn't want to see you."

Tears filled my eyes. I paid no attention to the guard's lies—but I had finally heard something about Dongwei! I felt his presence and was a little touched and excited.

After returning to the cell, everyone was envious that I'd had a chance to get out of the compound. They asked what had happened.

It is difficult to explain, but because of the daily ordeals, I had started to not miss Dongwei very much. Yet because of this incident, I missed him again, and my face was bathed in tears.

A practitioner surnamed Li sat by my side and asked me softly, "Missing home?"

I nodded. I immediately remembered that Li's husband was also imprisoned, and they also had a young child at home with no one to care for him. If I said I missed home, how would that make her feel?

I wiped my tears and forced a smile. "No, it's nothing. I'm fine now."

She smiled, and sighed. "The two of you aren't having it easy. But you have to be strong. Look at Aunt Qu—she's here with her three daughters!" I was really touched. Despite her suffering, she was still thinking of others.

There was a story involving Aunt Qu. Everyone heard about it. After learning that Uncle Qu and his three sons-in-law were not Falun Gong practitioners, the prison staff felt this was a great opportunity to "transform" the women by using their affection toward their husbands.

They summoned the four husbands and instructed them to persuade their wives to give up cultivation.

When the wives were brought to them, the four men instead raised their thumbs and said, "Persist!"

This caught the guards completely by surprise. In their fury, they told the men to leave immediately and pushed them out the prison door. But a guard-duty detainee had seen it, and the story was passed around the entire prison. Apparently, Aunt Qu's breast cancer was cured after she began cultivating, so the entire family supported Falun Dafa.

———•———

Once, a woman guard on duty called me over for a chat. At first, she asked why I practiced Falun Gong and why there were so many Falun Gong practitioners appealing to the authorities. I told her about the great physical and spiritual improvements I experienced after I began cultivating.

She sighed. "Why do you have to be so stubborn? Just write a guarantee statement, then do whatever you want when you get home!"

I told her that Falun Gong teaches Truthfulness, Compassion, and Tolerance. We couldn't lie. And wouldn't writing a guarantee be like agreeing that practicing Falun Gong is wrong, and that it's just fine for the CCP to arrest and torture practitioners? How could I say that?

She said, "Well, no matter how strong you think you are now, you'll think twice once you're taken to the labor camp."

I asked her if conditions in the labor camp were even worse than this place.

"Not worse, but—you'll see when you get there."

Even though I'd wanted to leave this horrible dispatch center for a long time, I had an inexplicable, chilling feeling when I thought about being taken to the labor camp. I told myself that no matter what happened, we had to persist in our belief.

———•———

One morning after about a month at the dispatch center, no one pushed us to begin work after breakfast. Instead, dozens of people's names were announced, and those people were told to pack their stuff. They were told that they were being taken to the labor camp. I was one of them.

I hurriedly packed my things, which consisted of quilts, pillow, sheet, clothing, towel, and toothbrush. Little Ren, the girl who had begun learning Falun Gong, looked at me with tears in her eyes. "Wait for me, Sister. I'll look for you when I get there and continue to cultivate with you."

The team leader also had tears in her eyes. "No one knows what will happen to all of you. Take care of yourselves!" I strongly suppressed my feelings and refused to cry.

Immediately after I finished packing, we were ordered to line up outside. About 50 people were taken to a small courtyard, and we were told to lower our heads, hug our arms and squat down. After a while, I heard a male voice say, "Male team, squat down here!"

"Male team?" My heart raced. Could Dongwei be there, too? Would we be taken together? Just before I could raise my head to take a look, a team leader barked, "Heads down!"

A while later, we were told to get up and walk toward the main gate. I glanced toward the male team to see if Dongwei was there. Alas, everyone was wearing the same clothes and had the same short haircut, so I could not tell at all.

Outside the gate, several large buses were waiting. We had to squat down, and they checked that everyone was there. I was glad that the male names were called first. I listened carefully but did not hear Dongwei's name. Were we going to be separated? Was he still staying in this cruel place?

On the way to the labor camp, the guards were nervous. We were not allowed to sit on the seats of the buses. Instead, we were made to squat beside them. All the window blinds were tightly sealed to prevent anyone from seeing us. Perhaps they didn't want others to know how many people were being taken to the labor camp. Were there people who still cared about us? I felt as though we had been forgotten by the world.

Within a short time, the bus arrived at Xin'an Labor Camp. The labor camp looked like the least likely place to hold prisoners, especially when compared to the Beijing Detention Center and the dispatch center. It had a nice door, and I could see a large compound with several ordinary-looking buildings. There were a lot of trees and flowers in the yard.

I wondered if this could be the place I had heard about, filled with horror and cleverly set traps.

CHAPTER NINE

September 27, 2000, is a day I will never forget. It was two months after I had been arrested, and I was taken to the Beijing Women's Xin'an Labor Camp. I was detained in the third of four groups. There were about 150 people to a group, and over 90 percent were Falun Gong practitioners.

There were about five or six hundred Falun Gong practitioners at the time I arrived. By the time I left, there would be a thousand. More and more Falun Gong practitioners would be brought in, and the camp would not be able to hold them all, so they would build the Beijing Female Labor Camp.

Upon my arrival, I was immediately subjected to a full body search and inspection of all my belongings. After that, sub-groups were formed. I was taken by the detainee on guard to a cell where I would be isolated. Anyone with a higher education, such as a master's degree or higher, was treated with much more "care" than less-educated practitioners.

There were six practitioners other than me with master's degrees. They were also subjected to special treatment, or as it was called, "intense surveillance." Jennifer Zeng was among the six. She was lucky to escape to Australia in 2001, and was featured in a documentary film called *Free China,* which has won many awards.

When I entered the cell, the detainees on guard looked me over carefully. I got the feeling that they were assessing their next target.

Then I could hardly believe my ears. I was told, "Go take a shower!"

Upon hearing these words, the feeling of someone who has not bathed in a month is indescribable. It also caught me off guard, and I suddenly felt warm all over. I thought, "Hey, this place is not so bad—they let you take showers!"

The shower was not all I had hoped for, however. There was no sprinkler, just a bucket to pour cold water over my body. For shampoo, I was given dish soap. For my body, a thick laundry detergent.

There was no way to untangle my hair, it was too far gone. When I washed it, chunks of hair fell out in my hands or rinsed out onto the ground. All the rest of my euphoria about being able to shower disappeared. My skin was red from the harsh detergent, and I still didn't feel clean.

Yet at least it was some kind of a "bath." I poured several buckets of cold water over myself. It was now late September, and my body trembled from the cold.

We would be allowed one bath per month.

After I was returned to the room, a guard brought in several people. Apparently, they wanted to "work on my thoughts." Everyone sat on a small stool, with me in the center.

This guard seemed a little different from the guards at the dispatch center—a bit kinder, and she seemed to want to reason things out with me.

At the dispatch center, I felt the guards were given no guidelines on how to torture people. Anything could happen at any time. Now it appeared that someone was willing to talk logically, and I was still willing as well. I also felt that as long as she was going to be reasonable, I would be able to explain the truth to her, because I am one who speaks the truth.

She asked how I was doing and inquired about my life. Then she told me that they knew Falun Gong practitioners are all good people who simply wish to follow Truthfulness, Compassion, and Tolerance. I could hardly believe my ears.

She said, "The nation is not against Truthfulness, Compassion, and Tolerance. Anyway, *Zhen-Shan-Ren* was not invented by Falun Gong. You can still live your life according to those principles even after you give up Falun Gong!"

I felt a murderous intention behind this "logic." To sever the connection between Falun Gong and its principles was a sinister and clandestine attempt to alter one's mind.

After more than a month of high-pressure torture at the dispatch center, my mind was a bit hazy. But having walked past the limit of survival, my wisdom was still intact.

"Okay, then," I countered. "If it's fine to follow Truthfulness, Compassion, and Tolerance, I'll make myself a T-shirt with the characters '*Zhen-Shan-Ren*,' and wear it around wherever I go. Is that okay?"

I had caught her off guard. She blurted out, "No, of course not! Everyone will realize it's Falun Gong. If you walk on the streets like that, we're still going to have to arrest you."

"There you go. Everyone knows that Falun Gong teaches Truthfulness, Compassion, and Tolerance. *Zhen-Shan-Ren is* Falun Gong. So your argument isn't valid. Even if I agreed to do what you said, the police would still arrest me because they equate Falun Gong with *Zhen-Shan-Ren*."

The guard paused for a long while, as if she was trying to figure out how to deal with me. Then she continued, "Many other religions also have similar teachings to *Zhen-Shan-Ren*. Buddhism and Christianity, for example. You can go study other religions. Why do you have to insist on this one?"

I thought about how everyone knows that the CCP teaches atheism. But in order to persecute Falun Gong, it has begun pulling people into other religions. Actually, the CCP also persecutes other religious people. But as long as you regard the Communist Party as Buddha's Buddha or God's God, then you can feel free to go to the temples and churches without upsetting the Party.

I thought to attack her reasoning from a different angle. "This may be hard to explain to an atheist, but I can give you a simple example. It's not a refined example, but I can't think of a better one. Let's say you are in love with someone, and he is in trouble. Someone else comes along and says to you, 'Why do you insist on loving this guy? Just let him go and fall in love with someone else! Look at the guy next door. He could be his look-alike because they are of the same height. Love him instead!' What would you think? Would you be able to immediately fall for him?"

She smiled. "Of course I would be able to fall in love with the other person, over time. It doesn't really matter if you love this or that person. Feelings can change."

I was speechless. "That is your attitude? I believe that loving someone is a binding of your heart and soul, due to many past lives together. How can you change your love like you change your clothes? For me, I want to go through thick and thin with my love. I will never part with the one I love."

She seemed a little embarrassed. "It's still early, there's no hurry. You'll understand with time." She stood up, looked at the other people surrounding me, and left.

One of the remaining people said, "Everyone says that Falun Gong has miraculous health effects. But it's actually all in the mind."

"Well, that would be all right, wouldn't it?" I said. "If it cures diseases, that's still a good thing for the nation and the family."

Another said, "Many people knew your Teacher before he publicized Falun Gong. He's just an ordinary person, and he only has a high school diploma."

"That's nothing unusual. I don't think Jesus was a college graduate. The Zen sect's sixth patriarch, Huineng, couldn't even read the most basic Chinese characters. Yet that doesn't prevent them from speaking the truth, or from knowing things that are beyond fundamental human abilities."

Another person tried to sound objective. "Falun Gong was very good to start with, but later its members began appealing to the government, handing out flyers, and they all became political."

"Who would appeal to the government if they weren't being persecuted?" I said. "And would there be a need to hand out flyers if appealing to the government were a viable option? Falun Gong has not changed. It has not participated in politics, either. It's protesting this irrational persecution. If one suffers injustice, shouldn't one speak up?"

Then another chimed in, "You dare to say that Falun Gong is not an organization?"

I replied, "Falun Gong is a loose group of people formed by many individuals. They come from all types of backgrounds, just like chess lovers often gather together to play chess. Would you call that an organization?"

As they began to repeat the same questions over and over, I finally started to catch on. They didn't want to discuss anything with me. Either they were repeating themselves senselessly on purpose, I thought, or they really weren't very bright. But of course it was intentional. They launched a constant assault to try to hit on some weakness they could expose. They would come at me from different angles, trying to find a way in.

Many hours passed until late at night. They didn't leave, nor did they stop talking.

I finally said, "All right, it looks like we have a communication problem. It's late. Why don't we go back and rest for now?"

One of them smiled a strange smile. He said with mock pleasantness, "Oh, no, it's no problem! None of us need to go to sleep! We can continue!"

I was so tired, I almost fell from the stool several times. They kept pulling me back up.

This went on until early morning. I saw light coming in through my window. I was so tired that I almost lost consciousness. All I could see was people coming closer, further, appearing or disappearing in front of me.

Their voices became slurred and I could no longer hear their words. I heard them say to let me sleep for two hours. Then I am not sure if I climbed into bed or they pulled me onto it. I was asleep immediately.

Not long afterward, they woke me up again and continued with this insane type of chat. The same few words repeated dozens, hundreds of times. The identities of the people seemed to change, but that didn't really sink in. Every minute seemed so long. Every minute was a minute spent breaking through a new limit in overcoming sleepiness.

Such psychological torture, on top of the filth and humiliation at the detention center, delivers tremendous blows to one's perseverance. Especially after being deprived of sleep for long periods of time, one's mind becomes weak.

Half-conscious, I did not realize that a campaign to annihilate my soul had already begun.

———•———

In the labor camp, "breaking the eagle" is a term used to describe forced deprivation of sleep. In the past, I wasn't sure why they called it "breaking the eagle" and not, for example, "breaking the cow," or "breaking the horse." It was only later that I found out that "breaking the eagle" is a real term. Sleep deprivation is one of the methods hunters use to tame eagles.

As the king of birds, the eagle's ability to soar high up, with its expansive view of the world, has made it the most unruly of birds. A male eagle that has just been caught will continuously attempt to break free from its shackles and return to the sky.

So the hunter will keep him hungry, thirsty, and struggling, under immense fatigue. Then, time and again, just when he is about to shut his eyes, the hunter will strike his head to make him unable to sleep.

When the eagle is incapable of withstanding the torture any longer and collapses, the hunter will douse him with cold water, and the cycle will be repeated. After enduring one night, an endless daytime will ensue. Even if the male eagle is as unyielding as before, his stature will be gradually weakened.

One day, two days, three days….

After being bitterly broken for three days, the hunter appears with clear water and mutton. By this time, fatigue, hunger, and despair have triumphed over the eagle's willpower, and it no longer rejects the hunter. It swallows the hunter's mutton with a grateful heart. The hunter is now the benefactor who has rescued him from his bitter predicament.

At the dispatch center, they first tortured my body and spirit to the extreme limit of endurance, and then brought me to the labor camp where they gave me a semblance of "breathing space." They continued to wear me down by not letting me sleep for a few days. After the body and spirit have become extremely frail, the "ideological remolding" begins.

In the labor camp, the police would constantly threaten Falun Gong practitioners with three choices. Be transformed, be tortured to death, or be forced to go mad.

For those who resolutely refused to be transformed in the labor camp, the horrible torture that they experienced far exceeds what humans can imagine. Often, when I think of them, my heart is filled with unspeakable grief.

A policewoman in the labor camp once personally told me, "Don't think you'll be exonerated after you have completed your one-year sentence. You will never be able to get out if you're not transformed."

"What reason do you have to keep me after my sentence ends?"

"We can extend your incarceration even after it expires. If we're unable to transform you after the first extension, there's always a second extension. Look at Zhao Ming.[14] Was his sentence not renewed twice?"

---

14 Zhao Ming is a Falun Gong practitioner who was a graduate student in Ireland when he was sentenced to a labor camp during a visit home in 1999. He was held at the Beijing Tuanhe Labor Camp and had his sentence extended twice. He was eventually released thanks to international pressure, but only after he agreed to renounce his belief during a torture session where he was shocked simultaneously with six electric batons.

I said, "Two extensions make up a year, but according to the regulations, you can only give up to a maximum of two extensions." Of course, re-education through labor is unconstitutional, but actually, the extension regulations I quoted were also illegal, as I would find out later.

She laughed coldly. "Don't think that the Party has no other methods. Now in the Northwest they are constructing special concentration camps for Falun Gong individuals. Those who do not get transformed will eventually be sent there, and it will be a point of no return for them."

I was sure she was only trying to scare me, and I didn't take her seriously.

———•———

Under the careful arrangement of the police in the labor camp, a practitioner I had known before, and who had my utmost trust, suddenly appeared one day. When I saw her, my heart brimmed with happiness.

I quickly went up to her and said, "Is it you? This is great! What on earth is going on here?"

She looked at me with a complex expression on her face. "We were wrong," she said. "We're too selfish!"

I was dumbfounded.

As Falun Gong practitioners, we had been the same as other people before we started cultivating. As judged by the principles of the universe, Truthfulness, Compassion, and Tolerance, we'd had a wealth of selfish motives and distracted thoughts.

But after learning Falun Gong, we understood that we came here to cultivate into selfless, enlightened beings who think of others before ourselves. We were getting better with practice, by virtue of a heart that unceasingly seeks to improve.

People in society, including policemen, cannot deny that Falun Gong practitioners are good. Practitioners refuse to take part in a life of indulgence, cheating, embezzlement, corruption, or harming others. Conversely, Falun Gong practitioners are largely honest, dependable, capable, and glad to help others.

"How are we selfish?" I blurted.

She rather excitedly and fervently replied, "Think about it. The Party has given us food and shelter and allowed us to be educated. Instead of being grateful after they give us so much, we repay their grace with enmity by resisting the Party and our country! How are we practicing 'Truthfulness, Compassion, Tolerance'? If we insist on practicing, giving our family members enormous pain, how are we being 'Compassionate'? Our Party forbids us to practice, yet we still disobediently persist in appealing for help, so where is our 'Tolerance'?"

At that time, I was similar to most Chinese, who were educated to make no distinction between the concepts of "country," "people," and "Party." It wasn't clear to me that the CCP only protects a ruler's personal interests and a ruling clique's benefits. They were using the power in their hands to force their will onto citizens, as a representative of the country, under the euphemistic term "serving the people."

From an early age, Chinese people are educated to imbibe concepts such as "Mother Party." The CCP plagiarizes the loving gratitude we have for our parents in Party songs, propaganda, and brainwashing textbooks. Back then, I could not detect the absurdity of this view.

In fact, the right to appeal is part of the original constitutional stipulations in China. This has now been labeled "resistance against the country," ever since the persecution of Falun Gong. The Party was acting against government laws by imprisoning and torturing Dongwei and me for writing letters.

A normal person assessing this situation would understand the serious errors of logic involved. But under the extreme environment in the labor camp, where my bodily suffering and mental humiliation made me despondent, I began to lose my self-confidence. My sense of judgment started to vacillate.

I started to question myself. Am I really without compassion and tolerance? If so, how can I say that I am practicing Falun Gong?

After noting my relative apprehension, she continued. "Thieves and robbers are guilty only of stealing and robbing things in this realm, but practitioners are dissatisfied with even the things in this realm and wish to obtain things from another realm! We are greedier than thieves! Don't think that you are so wonderful, because people like you are actually the worst kind around!"

What? I am worse than thieves and robbers? After hearing this, I blacked out and almost fainted. My self-confidence was utterly broken down, and I started to feel that I really had no merit. Could I really be that bad? Was I only practicing because of greed? After all, Master Li said that it is incorrect to practice with a heart of pursuit.

Because I had lost all powers of discrimination at that moment, I could not recognize this false logic that confused right and wrong, especially when I was faced with someone whom I knew and trusted. Of course, she had also been tortured until all her logic was gone. She was not conscious of the big logical loopholes in her words, and she believed that what she said was true.

The twisted logic and evil sayings continued to gnaw on my nerves. "If you are truly a good person, why are you here in jail? Aren't jails for the incarceration of bad people? You'd better do some proper reflection. Didn't Master Li say we should look within ourselves? In any case, we're obviously not doing something right!"

I started to follow her train of thought. Good people should not be in jail, yet I am jailed in a labor camp, so apparently I am not a good person. Master Li has said to search inside ourselves when we encounter difficulties. Does this mean that I am truly at fault? What is my problem?

Of course, we all know that there are innumerable historical examples of good people being incarcerated. When a leader with decision-making power has problems, it is possible to have a lot of unjust charges. For example, heroes like General Yue Fei, General Yang, and renowned ancient Chinese physician Hua Tuo had all been jailed.

A few years after leaving the labor camp, I would start to gradually realize that such rhetoric is the CCP's classic hoodlum logic.

My friend detected my doubts and confusion. "Listen," she said with sudden intensity. "This is a true test. Are you willing to give up what is most precious to you, for national interests?"

I immediately understood what she was implying and instinctively shouted, "No!" I gave her a panic-stricken look as I retreated a few steps.

"Why not?" she pressed. "Your unwillingness to give up shows that your selfish heart hasn't been removed!"

At the dispatch center, my body and spirit had suffered from immense pressure, but it had only come from outside. I had inherently understood that I was standing on the side of truth and justice.

But these lies and confused logic made me doubtful, deep down. Calling me "selfish" and "not truthful, not compassionate, not forbearing" were truly disintegrating my will from within.

Thereafter, they started to repeatedly hint that my psychology and spirit were not normal and that transformation was normal, because to resist transformation was to choose the single option of death. All around me in my surroundings, there were slogans such as "Transformation Gives New Life" and "Return to Human Nature."

They "regretfully and caringly" told me, "Do you know how frightening your looks are? Many paranoids look just like this. Of course you don't know. How many mad people admit that they are insane? You think that imprisoning some Falun Gong practitioners in asylums is persecuting them? They actually really are insane. And isn't it real nobility if you can truly give up your most precious thing for your country?"

I tried to focus my thoughts so as to distinguish the veracity or falseness of these speeches, but the thoughts fluttered suddenly, as if they were in an illusory space. My heart was filled with enormous fear, a fear that my will would scatter with the wind and my spirit would split.

I was not sure how long this besiegement lasted, but they must have finally noticed that I was on the verge of collapse, because they granted me the "gracious gift" of a short rest. However, I was completely unable to go to sleep because by this time I had been broken down to such an extent. I crawled into bed and cried incessantly, my tears soaking the pillow.

I repeatedly asked, "Master Li, what should I do? Am I really selfish? Am I really not taking my country into consideration? Do I really need to take this step?"

I felt I must be on the brink of a breakdown.

————◆————

The darkest days of my life were the days of torture in the labor camp, which brought me to the verge of several mental breakdowns, when I was deceived and forced to give up my practice. Those dark days were accompanied by shame, a sense of betrayal, despair, an indescribably bitter pain, a death-in-life. Due to my overwhelming pain and regret, even when I later became sober-minded, I had lost the confidence to continue practicing.

Later, I discovered that a huge government apparatus had deceived me using the most sinister methods. An indescribable sense of anger and sadness came over me after I understood what had happened.

Why did I believe those lies? Upon careful reexamination, I discovered that, apart from my character as a practitioner and my relative immaturity at that time, there were two more reasons.

The first reason was my vague understanding of the true nature of the CCP back then. I didn't think it was capable of designing such shockingly devious schemes. Before reading the *Nine Commentaries on the Communist Party*,[15] based on my history of reading and the knowledge I had acquired, I was fundamentally unable to truly understand the CCP.

Although my parents were from the generation that had lived through the Cultural Revolution, out of a loving wish to protect me, they never told me about such things. My parents had suffered a lot in their lifetimes, and due to their single-minded wish to make their children happy, they had always assumed that profusely doting on me in every possible way would fulfill that wish.

I had never been interested in politics, so I thought the CCP's influence on me was minute. But I had seriously underestimated the brainwashing education I had received since kindergarten.

This "Party culture" is analogous to the air that pervades the entire land of China. It is impossible to escape contamination, because the population is soaked in it, from primary school through university. Besides our textbooks, teaching materials, and exam questions, even films, television, music, and dance all contain elements of Party culture.

This type of indoctrination is so systematic, so detailed, and so omnipresent that I was not cognizant of the fact that many of my ideas were a direct result of the brainwashing.

It is only now, after reading the *Nine Commentaries on the Communist Party* many times, along with a book called *Disintegrating the Party Culture,* that I finally understand why I was still using the CCP's way of thinking to ponder over issues, even at the brink of death while in their hands.

For example, the issue that made me most miserable in the process of my "transformation" was the question of whether I could give up what was most precious to me for national interests. The question itself is a fabrication created by Party culture.

The CCP intentionally confuses the relationship between Party, nation, and the people in it. It wants to become the "Mother Party,"

---

15 *Nine Commentaries on the Communist Party* is a series of editorials published in 2004 by the Epoch Times, an independent Chinese newspaper. Drawing upon official sources and personal testimony, it offers an uncensored analysis of the CCP's history and reign, including the estimated 80 million deaths it caused as of 2004. Its publication sparked a wave of millions of Chinese people symbolically renouncing their association with the Party and its related youth organizations. The Party has gone to great lengths to limit the *Nine Commentaries'* distribution inside China, including arresting those thought to be circulating it. www.ninecommentaries.com

that is, the living "incarnation" of the country and the people. Often we had to loudly sing "Oh Party, beloved Mother," and we were taught to feel that disobedience to the Party was synonymous with betraying national interests.

In actuality, giving up our faith in *Zhen-Shan-Ren* was the real betrayal of the interests of our country and people. So many Falun Gong practitioners have obtained purification and elevation of their bodies, minds, and souls. They have thus supported the country not only through a large reduction of medical expenses, but also through family harmony and contributions to society through a conscientious work ethic. These are the real national and people's interests.

But back then, the relationship between country, people, and Party was jumbled in my mind. I equated the Party's will with the country's will and even perceived it as higher than all of our individual wills. This phenomenon is widespread in our generation of young people. I've seen that even students who are studying overseas still adhere to this.

Later, when I would study at Cambridge, I'd attend a gathering of Chinese students and relate the bitter experiences that Dongwei and I had suffered. A postgraduate professorial candidate from mainland China unexpectedly said to me, "No matter how much your mother beats you, she's still your mother. How can you relate such incidents to foreigners? Shouldn't you take our country's image into consideration?"

Truly, in the past, I would have swallowed my own tooth if the Party had knocked it out while beating me, for fear of being branded with the infamous labels of "disloyal" or "impious." It is only now that I finally understand the distinction between China as a country with a culture of five thousand years, and the Party, with its mere 60 years of control. How can the CCP be the "mother" of the Chinese people?

The CCP is not China, so criticizing the CCP is definitely not criticizing China. In fact, it is the CCP's actions that have truly spoiled the image of China.

The second reason I was deceived was my lack of legitimate education in traditional culture, and influences from a young age that resulted in some flaws in my personality. My parents and the people in their generation had experienced the Cultural Revolution that destroyed traditional culture, and after that, they simply didn't know what type of truths or methods to use to educate their children.

Growing up under the indoctrination of the CCP, the only facets of me that were not molded by it were my belief in God and my kind personality. I am someone who innately believes in God. No matter how I was educated since I was little to refute the existence of God, I have never doubted the existence of God.

As a graduate student, I remember discussing this issue with a schoolmate. She said with surprise, "I really cannot imagine that a twentieth century modern youth like you would still be so 'idealistic.'"

"But God exists objectively," I told her, "and therefore belongs to the 'material' category!"

Perhaps it was my belief in the existence of God and my good natural disposition that enabled me to feel comfortable right away with Falun Gong.

Before cultivation, my greatest dream was to pursue a romantic and enduring love. My period of romance with Dongwei was the most important thing in my life. I also read love stories. I was often inescapably absorbed in them.

I should say that the CCP encourages young people to develop in this manner, because people who are wholeheartedly immersed in matters of the heart won't be too interested in ideas of democracy and freedom.

Ancient China's traditional culture spoke of justice, humanity, and moral courage. Many loyal ministers and chivalrous people once steadfastly embraced the philosophy of "better to make jade and be shattered than to make tiles to protect oneself." That is, they would rather die than surrender when faced with threats or bribes, for example. Such moral boundaries are remote to my generation, and my personality lacks such tenacity.

Due to these "historical" reasons, with the labor camp breaking me to my limit by depriving me of sleep, and the CCP's historically unprecedented methods of deception, the innocent me was no match for it. After a series of tortures to my spirit, I was, in the absence of my good senses, "transformed." I signed a statement which claimed I would not practice Falun Gong.

Falun Gong practitioners who have been transformed can all attest to the same experience. The first thing the guards insist on after we have been brainwashed is that we communally sing a song called "The Same Song."

"The Same Song" was originally a pop song in China that was converted into a tool for torture, and then proudly made into a patriotic song used for propaganda. A variety show was created by the same name, using "The Same Song" as its theme song. Though the lyrics seem cheerful and innocuous, the song and the show have been used in various propaganda campaigns, along with songs such as, "Let Me Sing a Song to the Party," and "Follow the CCP Wherever it Goes."

Having to sing this song felt like being forced to laugh heartily at a loved one's funeral. It was really brutal and strange. I excused myself from their joyous celebration by saying that I lacked musical sense and would sing out of tune, yet they insisted on singing by my side for me to hear.

After experiencing a nightmarish period of immense pressure, suddenly hearing this "sweet and melodious" song was rather like the nail in the coffin of the soul. I felt a strong sense of wanting to be extricated from it all. My only thought was: "Let all this be over quickly. Let all the pain go away and never be mentioned again. Let all this end, lest I really go mad."

After that, I went and hid, weeping bitterly for a few hours until I lost all sense of my surroundings. I felt only an unspeakable grief and despair as I continuously said to myself in my heart, "I cannot practice. I cannot practice for life."

Later, a fellow inmate told me, "You scared us when you cried so hard! We've never seen anyone grieve so much. We were really afraid when you lost your voice. How are you going to go on after your heart has been broken to such an extent?"

The pain I experienced was so severe and grave that I couldn't remember Dongwei and the sweet times we had spent together. My spirit was in a state of hazy confusion for a long time. I couldn't even remember who I was. Everything was so distant, and the world outside the labor camp was so far away. It was as if only the labor camp was real and this "real world" could only bring despair.

CHAPTER TEN

Under the sealed, extreme environment of the labor camp, my nerves gradually became numb. It was like the old fairy tale from India: An ugly demon wished for a beautiful princess to fall in love with it, but it knew that was unlikely. So it kidnapped the princess and forbade her to have contact with normal people.

The demon talked to the princess every day but wouldn't allow her to see it. As time went on, in the princess's state of helpless isolation and vulnerability, she soon grew accustomed to the demon's voice. Then the demon revealed a claw for the princess to see. After she got used to seeing the claw, it revealed a second claw. Eventually, the princess got used to the whole demon, and she began a life with it.

The CCP uses similar methods to force Falun Gong practitioners to give up their faith. They even organized a conference with experts so they could learn the latest results of psychological research that might be useful for transforming Falun Gong practitioners. This repeated brainwashing that distorts the facts is still an important tactic in the persecution.

Psychological research into contemporary advertising has indicated that images and words that appear repeatedly form an impression on a person's cerebral cortex after they are viewed seven times or more. This happens whether or not the person has paid attention to or believed in the subject matter at the time. If they appear more than 40 times, a person starts to think that what the advertisements say is his own understanding.

This is why so many Chinese people nowadays (including overseas Chinese) who have never read Falun Gong literature or interacted with Falun Gong practitioners have a negative impression of the practice. It is a result of the massive vilification and propaganda campaign launched by state media after July 20, 1999. Many people still have not realized that this is intentional indoctrination and not their own thoughts about Falun Gong.

The policemen in the labor camp also used whatever lies they could think of against us. They would hold *Zhuan Falun* in their hands for us to see and say that they were also Falun Gong practitioners, but that it was now time to give it up.

It must have been really hard for those policemen to pretend to be good people in front of us. They tried to act like they had already cultivated to a high level. For example, the education Section Chief frequently demonstrated his presumed learned and selfless side in front of me. For the lofty purpose of transforming and salvaging Falun Gong practitioners, he immersed himself in the labor camp every day and didn't even go home.

Not long after I got out of the labor camp, I heard something about the Section Chief. A man I knew wanted to develop good relations with him, hoping he might help free the man's wife from the labor camp. Taking full advantage of the situation, the Section Chief requested that he find a young lady for him. It was a big shock to me when I found out about this. A true Falun Gong practitioner would never do something like this.

Still later, I found that the policemen in the labor camps made their income in a different way than those in police stations, who made a lot of their money from shady, unethical sources. The labor camp police had once held jobs with extremely low wages and benefits. Now at the labor camps, they could obtain a large bonus for every Falun Gong practitioner they transformed. Thus, their level of enthusiasm was high, and they would even neglect sleeping and eating for the sake of making money.

The "godless" doctrine that the CCP brainwashes Chinese people with from a young age is one reason why those policemen would dare to do such things. Traditionally in Chinese history, people who led pious lives were regarded with extra respect. Even the general populace devoutly respected Buddha and the universe. Such people could never have committed such cruel and revolting deeds.

Another reason the police dared to do this was the CCP's control of the government and even the judges. With the CCP securely behind them, the policemen became fearless.

The CCP's policy against Falun Gong—from an order given by Jiang Zemin, the head of state at the time—is to "Destroy their reputations, exhaust them financially, and eliminate them physically." In addition, "Beaten to death can be counted as suicide," and "Cremate immediately. No need to verify name or residence."

Why is the CCP so afraid of Falun Gong practitioners? I puzzled over this for a long time. It was only after I read the Fifth Commentary in the *Nine Commentaries on the Communist Party*, years later, that I understood why the CCP launched such a brutal persecution against Falun Gong.

Falun Gong teaches truthfulness, compassion, and tolerance, while the Communist Party brews falsehood, hatred, and struggle. So from an ideological point of view, the philosophy that the Communist Party has relied on for its survival is the polar opposite of what Falun Gong teaches.

The CCP relies on fear to maintain its political power. But how can it control a group that can't be bribed or threatened into committing wrongdoing, whose practitioners uphold high moral standards regardless of external influences? As more and more people would come to recognize and embrace the goodness of *Zhen-Shan-Ren*, it would naturally follow that they would reject the Party's philosophy.

——— • ———

One day I was requested to write down my feelings after being "transformed." It was an autumn afternoon, and I was sitting on a small stool, leaning against a little window. My head was blank, and I could not write anything. I could only see the golden sun rays shining on the piece of paper that I had on my lap.

Suddenly I heard a thunderclap outside the window I was leaning on. This was immediately followed by an enormous sound, after which approximately ten sounds of mellow thunder ensued, and then the sound gradually vanished into a distant place. Along with the dissipating thunderclap, I felt my consciousness gradually becoming blurred as I instantly had an extremely frightening thought. "My soul has left me!"

Panic-stricken, I asked those near me, "Did you hear that thunder?"

No one had heard it, and they gave me strange looks. Was I really the only person who had heard the sound? What was it? Had my soul really left me? If my soul had indeed left, what use did I still have for my physical body?

From that day on, I was often caught in a stupefied state. I was in the world, but not in it. Time and again, I would suddenly ask those around me, "Do you see me? Do you recognize me?" I was so afraid I was going insane.

———•———

In the labor camps, practitioners who refused to renounce their belief suffered excruciating physical and mental pain. After a period of brainwashing, practitioners who had not been transformed would be taken to an "Intensive Training Unit" (ITU), where they were cruelly tortured.

This unit is in an isolated courtyard, located at the left side of Beijing Xin'an Labor Camp. There are several single-level small buildings that look just like ordinary houses. The brutality suffered by practitioners there is terrifying. Those who experienced it told me that although you didn't die, a layer of skin would be ripped off.

Practitioners in the ITU would be isolated in a 3- to 4-square-meter, windowless room. They had to eat, sleep, and relieve themselves in there. They could not leave this cell without special permission.

The cell held a stone bed, a faucet, and a toilet. In winter, practitioners could have a light quilt, but no mattress. The winter in Beijing is usually below zero degrees Celsius, reaching 20 below at its coldest. The cells were extremely cold, as there was no heating facility. Even seniors 60 or 70 years old had to sleep on the ice-cold stone beds.

Actually, opportunities to lie down were few. Most of the time, practitioners were forced to stand facing the wall at night, sometimes from several hours to more than ten. Frequently, they were permitted to sleep for only two or three hours a night.

The meals never changed—two fist-sized, stone-hard steamed corn buns and a bowl of soup without vegetables.

A young female practitioner I met at the labor camp described her suffering in the ITU. She was forced to stand facing the wall for ten or more hours. She said it was impossible for a person who had not eaten nutritious food and who suffered from severe sleep deprivation to stand so long. She couldn't remember how many times she almost collapsed when standing in front of the wall. If she had not held her strong belief in her heart, she would have fallen to the ground.

She also told me they considered it a blessing when they could stand without being harassed. Much of the time, a group of people surrounded them, deliberately fraying their nerves and battering their minds with theories and talk designed to confuse them. That was much worse, and the most horrifying result was that one might come to accept their theories. At that point, they were close to becoming insane from this type of torture.

Besides sleep deprivation and brainwashing, the practitioners in ITU suffered even crueler forms of torture. They were kept isolated, so no one knew of the torture they endured. I heard about these things only after I was released, but I remember in the labor camp seeing a young girl whose face was terribly blistered.

Another young female practitioner described how the guards shocked her with electric batons. She said that at one time, four or five guards shocked her at the same time. They pressed the electric batons to her face, head, forehead, neck, and the back of her hands without stopping.

She felt a strong electric current passing through her entire body. Blue sparks flew around her, stinging fiercely and tearing through her body. She said it felt just like viper fangs piercing her. She clenched her teeth together tightly to withstand the excruciating pain.

Her heart beat fiercely, and she felt she could no longer endure it. She had a hard time breathing, as her trachea became irritated.

The right part of her face was covered with a one-centimeter-thick blister, without a single spot of healthy skin. Blisters covered her back, hands, and neck, and pus drained out of the blisters for days. A scab formed later, covering the entire right part of her face.

Some of the guards in the labor camps are mentally deranged and sadistic. They have a preference for shocking pretty, young female practitioners' faces.

There are many practitioners who were disfigured after being shocked with electric batons.

One practitioner, Gao Rongrong, a beautiful lady from Shenyang Province, was completely disfigured after five hours of continuous shocks to her face with electric batons. Her suffering has alarmed people who have seen photos of her, which were taken secretly by another practitioner who was visiting her in the hospital ten days after the torture. She died shortly after the photos were taken.

There are many others who suffered a similar fate, but whose stories haven't been revealed because of the Party's information blockade.

Gao Rongrong

At the end of 2000, the Communist Party's Central Committee started holding "brainwashing classes" in labor camps. Many Falun Gong practitioners who worked for the central government were sent to these brainwashing classes.

A lady I knew, Ge Cuibo, was a staff member at the National Audit Office of China. She was arrested at home while still in her pajamas.

When she was sent to the labor camp, she refused to get out of the car to attend the brainwashing class. Seven or eight police officers dragged her and carried her to the class. She didn't make it easy for them—it took them a long time to get her in there.

We saw the entire incident when she arrived. The policemen

guards saw the surprised look on our faces, and one of them said, "See? Practitioners who can't be 'transformed' are mentally ill! Don't you think so? They arrive in their pajamas and refuse to get out of the car." The guards laughed.

The policeman even dared to add, "Can't you see that they are helpless without us? It's our responsibility to stop them from making fools of themselves. Don't you think so?"

I was speechless. Only later did I really realize how preposterous this was. It was obvious that Ms. Ge Cuibo had been arrested at night and had not been allowed to dress.

Ge Cuibo was arrested again after I left China. No one knows her whereabouts now.

I remember another practitioner, Ms. Zhang Yijie, a section director from the Ministry of Commerce. Officers from the Security Bureau arrested her inside the government compound in broad daylight. I met her once in the labor camp. She was a gentle, quiet, elegant lady with a strong will. She resisted the persecution and went on a hunger strike when taken to the brainwashing class.

I heard that she was later sentenced to two years of forced labor at Xin'an Labor Camp, where she suffered cruel torture. She was forced to stand outdoors in the cold of winter for 42 days and nights, wearing only underwear. Because of continued physical torture, her vertebra became dislocated, and there were injuries all over her body. When she was released she looked very old. Her hair had turned white and her teeth had become loose. Ms. Zhang wrote a fascinating account of her experiences:
http://en.minghui.org/emh/articles/2007/2/17/82766p.html

In the labor camp, I once overheard police guards talking about a special team that had been formed to do research on how best to make practitioners renounce Falun Gong. They were looking for weaknesses to exploit.

They concluded that practitioners who are committed to cultivating themselves always want to be altruistic and kind-hearted. Therefore, they decided that scolding them for being selfish and unkind would be a useful psychological tool. This would lead to loss of confidence in one's cultivation.

So they began to repeatedly tell practitioners, "You are being very selfish! Your family has been ruined because of your practice. Why do you isolate yourself here in the labor camp, when you should be contributing to society?"

When I realized their intentions, I thought, "They are doing this type of mental torture systematically and intentionally. We have to remain firm and not be affected by these machinations."

But in such an evil environment, such clear thoughts were like a splash. They came one moment and disappeared the next. My brain, filled with ever more lies, became too disordered to sort it out anymore.

———◆———

Time passed very slowly in the labor camp. The only bright light was that my colleagues would occasionally come to visit me. A young girl who joined the company the same year I did had become a close friend of mine. She burst into tears the first time she saw me in the labor camp. I felt that she saw my circumstances and pitied me.

But other colleagues were also bursting into tears when they visited, and I wasn't sure why. One day I caught a glimpse of myself in a mirror, and I saw how much I had changed. I didn't recognize myself even after looking in the mirror for a long time. I saw an image of a lady with rough skin, lightless eyes, and a puffy, lifeless face.

I had never cared too much about my appearance. Dongwei and I had been together for many years, and since he didn't usually pay attention to what I looked like, I had let myself go a bit. I had never thought of myself as especially beautiful. But I do have regular features and bright shining eyes. After practicing Falun Gong, my skin began to feel like silk. Was the lady in the mirror really me? Now I understood why my colleagues had burst into tears. After seeing the changes in me, I couldn't calm down for a long time.

One time, one of my female colleagues secretly gave me a bottle of moisturizing lotion (cosmetics were not allowed in the camp) and told me to use it daily. But I stopped after I had used it a few times because when I tried to rub it on my face, it was painful. It was like trying to smooth out sandpaper.

Later my colleagues no longer broke out in tears when they saw me. Maybe they'd gotten used to how I looked. But they were worried and told me repeatedly, "Pay attention to your psychological health." I didn't understand what they meant.

After I came back to work, a colleague told me why they had been worried about it. In the days before my detention, in their eyes, I was a smart and confident girl who was a great asset to the office. I was intelligent and could easily analyze the international economy.

But when I was in the labor camp, they saw I was unkempt and wearing oversized labor camp clothes. They saw me being forced to stand at attention and "report" whenever I saw the guards and policewomen. They knew me well and were worried that I might be driven to madness under such conditions.

What my colleagues feared really did happen to another imprisoned practitioner, my good friend Yang Yan. She used to go to our practice site at Purple Bamboo Park before the persecution. She was the one in our study group who wore the Falun Gong pin and told me to be strict with myself.

Though we were imprisoned in the same labor camp, Yang Yan and I were in different sections. We didn't get a chance to talk to each other but nodded our heads when we occasionally saw each other at a distance.

Rumor had it that she suffered tremendously at the camp and almost died when guards force-fed her. One time, she was shocked brutally with electric batons because she had done the Falun Gong exercises. She was also forced to take care of an elderly lady at the camp who had suffered a mental collapse because of being tortured. Yang Yan had to care for her day and night, getting no sleep.

I saw her after I was released. Her physical body was a mess, and she had mental problems. She could no longer communicate properly, so no one could find out exactly how she had been tortured and driven to such a state. Forthright and generous young Yang Yan had been turned into a listless and unresponsive middle-aged-looking woman who sat with a blank expression on her face. Seeing her, my heart broke to pieces.

———— • ————

Not a day passed in the forced labor camp when I didn't feel deep pain and despair. I wasn't allowed to know anything about Dongwei. At the beginning, I used to think of him a lot. But after some time in that evil environment without any spiritual sustenance, I became numb and no longer even missed him.

I tried to hold onto the thought that I could not lose my consciousness and that I had to keep my sanity. My mind told me that as long as I could hold onto these thoughts, Dongwei and I might be reunited.

When I thought about Dongwei having to suffer the same fate, the same torture and mistreatment, it was deeply painful to my heart.

After the loud thunder-like noise that only I could hear, I became numb and behaved like a zombie. I felt like a walking corpse. One scenario from a German movie I had seen some time before held my mind captive.

German movies were more difficult for me to understand than European movies, but I was often surprised at the deep meanings I found in certain scenes.

Watching movies had always been one of my hobbies. I was fascinated by European movies, especially movies based on British classical masterpieces, such as Jane Austen's *Sense and Sensibility* or *Pride and Prejudice*, or Charles Dickens' *A Tale of Two Cities*. These movies had an antique flavor, and I never got tired of watching them.

Actually, China has a very strict censorship system regarding foreign movies—many interesting films would never be permitted there. But people can still buy DVDs of foreign movies at some semi-underground video stores at a low price—about $2 to $5. The quality of those DVDs is usually quite poor.

I can't recall the name of the movie that was on my mind in the labor camp, but I remember it depicted a demon in the appearance of a handsome man who came to the human world. He met a country girl who was very poor but of pure character and kind heart. He wanted to buy the girl's soul for a million dollars.

The girl was not interested, so the demon raised the amount. The girl told him that her refusal was not based on the price he offered, but on the fact that one cannot live without one's soul.

A man overheard the conversation and followed the demon. "You want to buy a soul, right? Buy mine, please. Mine is cheaper—only a hundred thousand dollars."

The demon replied, "But your soul isn't worth anything at all."

As that scene came back to me in the labor camp, I felt so afraid that I had unconsciously sold my soul to a demon.

CHAPTER ELEVEN

In early 2001, my colleagues told me that I might be released soon because my workplace had put pressure on the labor camp staff. A light of hope shimmered in my heart.

Daily life at the camp was filled with suffering. Every day, besides attending the brainwashing classes, we were forced to do hard labor, such as planting trees, weeding on the grounds, and knitting exported sweaters.

In spite of these hardships, though, I felt much better thinking I might be leaving that monster's den soon. I started smiling again.

Most everyone is slightly unstable when the moment of freedom finally approaches. It lifts the spirit and warms the heart because there is no one who does not want to leave such a place. Everyone counts the minutes and holds hope in their hearts.

Several days before I was released, a camp guard came to talk to me. My mind was not clear, and I told her that I knew that I was not a good person and I would try to do better. She thought for a moment and said, "You are not bad. In fact, you are just too conscientious. Changing a little to the opposite might be good for you."

I was dumbfounded. It seemed she was telling me not to cave in, to not accept the transformation, that it had only been a method to achieve a goal. Yet, for practitioners, it represents the death of their soul. What was going on? Actually, I saw and experienced much that made me doubt that transformation was the right thing.

For one thing, illnesses were reappearing in practitioners who were transformed.

The mystery was that every time I had clear thoughts like this, they disappeared soon after they appeared. I asked myself "Why?" Sometimes I heard a voice in my mind, "Since you chose this path, you have to continue walking it." It was as if something controlled my mind and I had no say in the matter.

I begged a colleague to inquire about Dongwei. I was wondering if he also would be released and if I would see him again. My colleague inquired and told me that they would not release him at this time, as he had just been taken to Tuanhe Labor Camp. He had been detained at the horrible dispatch center for a long time.

Dongwei's company had sent his colleagues to visit him several times. The staff at the dispatch center realized this was a prosperous company, so they held Dongwei as a hostage and demanded a ransom. Dongwei suffered there from summer until winter.

It was summer when I was held at the dispatch center, and the heat and filth were unbearable. Later I learned that it was even worse in winter because of the extreme cold. The clothing they provided was not warm, so everyone shivered through the cold winter weather. Food had to be eaten fast, or it would start to freeze.

Labor during the winter was also harder, and it was more difficult to wrap chopsticks. Everyone was forced to work harder and longer. Often, they were not allowed to go to sleep until around 6 a.m., when it was time to start work for the next day. Even during breaks or before starting to work on another product, they were not allowed to go indoors and have some rest. Instead, the guards forced them to practice parading in the cold wind. Many times, people fell to the ground unconscious because of hunger and cold.

Although I knew I would not see Dongwei immediately after my release, the hope of reunion with my parents comforted me a little. My parents came to see me only a few times at the labor camp. It was not easy for them to come to Beijing because they lived thousands of miles away.

A caged person definitely desires to see his or her family. But I could not bear to have my aged parents traveling back and forth, especially since they were so anguished to see me in this condition. My heart broke seeing my parents suffer like this.

My parents were always proud of Dongwei and me because we excelled at school and at our jobs. When they heard that we had both been imprisoned, it was as if the sky had collapsed.

The first time when I saw my parents at the labor camp, I saw their aged looks and worried eyes through the thick window. I felt that their suffering was no less than ours.

I heard later that when my parents were told of our arrest, my father lost all his strength and nearly fell to the ground, and my mother felt as if half of her had died. They were also furious at our unjust suffering in the labor camp.

I had always been the apple of my parents' eyes, and they treated me like a queen. Knowing this, I could not tell them the truth about the cruel torture we suffered in the labor camp. Even though they had lived through the Cultural Revolution and must have understood something of the horror of the CCP, they could never have guessed the extent of the inhuman mental and physical torture we suffered. And I could not tell them—I was afraid the truth would kill them.

———•———

Finally the day of my release arrived, the day I had waited for with high hopes and dreamed of day and night. That morning, I gave my belongings to poor people in the labor camp. No one was paid anything for their hard labor. On the contrary, inmates at the labor camp had to pay for everything they needed, even their work tools—small wooden stools, meal boxes, and so on. Inmates whose families have no money to deposit into their accounts at the labor camp have a very difficult time.

After breakfast, I decided to help my team fill the boiled water for the last time. All the people in charge of filling the drinking water gathered in the water room, including members of the fourth team.

Right away I saw Little Ren! She is the young girl convicted of drug addiction whom I had taught Falun Gong to at the dispatch center. In fact, she had been at the labor camp for a while already, but we hadn't met because we were in different teams. I never imagined I would meet her the day I was to be released. I took this as a sign that we were meant to meet again.

She ran toward me quickly and said impatiently, "Sister! I kept inquiring about you from the day I arrived. I am told that you will be released soon. I just have one question. Should I continue to practice Falun Gong?'"

I didn't know how to respond. After a moment's silence, I asked her, "How do you feel after learning it?"

"Well, after you left, my enemy reported on me." Reporting on others' crimes results in reduction of one's penalty. She continued, "Normally, I would risk my life to fight her! But I recalled Teacher's words that you told me, '*A benevolent person always has a heart of compassion. With no discontentment or hatred, he takes hardship as joy.*' That calmed me down. Later, I recited this again and again. In the end, I didn't hate her anymore. It was so amazing!"

After she said that, it was just as if my mind was opened and I knew what to say. "Go ahead and practice it secretly. It's good for everyone if you become a better person." She nodded as if relieved of a heavy load and said, "Sister, I'm relieved after hearing your opinion. But why did they say that you stopped practicing it?"

I hesitated for a while and said, "It's not the case, actually." I let out a sigh. "That's a long story. Let's talk about it when we have a chance to meet again outside of here."

She nodded her head with a pitying look in her eyes and reluctantly returned to her queue.

I was anxious to return home, but the procedures were complicated. Being afraid that prisoners would try to keep in contact with each other once they were released, they did a body search. They wanted to make sure I didn't take anyone's letters or phone numbers with me. The procedures went on and on. Not until the afternoon did I walk out the black gate, the leaving I had dreamed of for many days and nights.

The feeling when I walked out of the labor camp gate is something difficult to describe. The strain of not being quite certain it was for real was hard on me. I thought, "Have I really been released from that hell in the human world, that horrible den of demons?"

I was worried that it was just a dream. I exerted all my strength to overcome this despair. I pinched my arm hard. The more painful it felt, the happier I was.

I imagined that my parents would be waiting impatiently for me. How I wanted to run into their arms!

But sadly, only some colleagues were waiting for me. They looked as if they were ready to face a formidable enemy. They had no experience picking people up from labor camps.

Although I was happy to see them, I couldn't stop myself from asking, "Where are my parents? Where are they?"

"They're waiting for you at home," someone said. "We have to go to the police station to report before you can go home. We have no idea how long this will take, so we just asked them to stay at home."

What? I was just released from the labor camp and now the police were waiting for me? I was completely perplexed. "Why is that?" I asked. "Do all released labor camp inmates have to go to the police station?"

"Falun Gong practitioners do. Don't think too much about it. It's better than staying in the labor camp, isn't it?"

I followed them reluctantly to the police station. When the police asked me to sign a document consenting to their surveillance afterward, I felt the blood rushing to my face. The happiness I felt after escaping from the hell of the labor camp completely disappeared after I heard their unreasonable and lawless request. The feeling of despair returned. Would I ever be rid of the devil's grip?

Later, a friend who worked at the National Security Department told me that individuals like Falun Gong practitioners would be monitored for 50 years by the government. The expense for such surveillance, of course, would come from ordinary citizens' sweat and toil.

Night had already fallen when we left the police station. Walking toward my home, I saw two white-haired elderly ladies standing in the wind. One was my mother and the other was my mother-in-law.

My mother and Dongwei's mother took me in their arms and held me tightly. Tears of happiness ran down their faces.

They were so sentimental that at first they didn't notice my colleagues. My coworkers couldn't help but cry too, during this emotional moment. It took these two elderly ladies a few minutes before they remembered to thank my coworkers. Then we walked home, holding hands and wiping our tears.

I had finally come back to the home I'd dreamed of while I was being tortured and mistreated. I was back in the arms of those dear ones I had missed for so long. But happiness eluded me, and I felt as though I were living in a dream.

My mother's loving eyes took in my appearance. She couldn't hold back her tears. My mother-in-law was also thinking of her beloved son when she saw telltale signs of the torture I had suffered. It almost broke her heart. She hugged me tightly, crying large tears that would not stop.

My father and father-in-law broke up the emotional scene by

asking us to come and eat dinner. It was a relief for me, as I was at a loss. I had no way to console these two dear ladies.

After a simple and crude breakfast in the labor camp, I had not had a chance to eat anything and was quite hungry. My father and father-in-law had outdone themselves cooking dinner—all my favorite dishes. The four of them just kept watching me eat, so I had to tell them that the food was delicious.

In fact, I had lost my sense of taste. I might as well have been eating wax. It was rather troubling, and I worried that I wouldn't be able to recapture anything from my past.

After dinner, I wanted to take a shower. I had not taken one for an entire month, and that shower had been with cold water, and with others watching, so I had rushed through it.

What a feeling! I could finally take a warm shower at my own speed, with real soap, in my own bathroom.

I enjoyed the shower tremendously and was reluctant to turn the water off. Then I remembered the water shortage in Beijing and thought about Master Li saying to be good. I turned off the water and got out.

I had hoped for some relaxation, but it really wasn't possible because I had to pretend to be happy and carefree in front of my family. Otherwise, the atmosphere would be too oppressive for any of us. It was not easy to be lighthearted, so I covered myself with a quilt when it was still early in the evening.

The quilt was soft and warm. I smelled a delicate fragrance that helped me feel that I had truly escaped the labor camp. Yet I was sleepless, remembering the visit to the police station immediately after being released. I was also saddened because I could see that my parents and parents-in-law had aged by ten years.

Knowing that Dongwei was still suffering in that horrible labor camp, I wanted to cry my heart out. I held myself in check and did not cry because I thought it would make our parents feel worse than they already did. It was so difficult to refrain from crying and to not give way to my feelings of despair. The quilt was like a security blanket and helped stop my emotions from coming out. But my body shook violently with suppressed emotion.

Dongwei would not be released from the labor camp for a few more months. Living without him was heartbreaking. My daily routine consisted of working, eating, sleeping. I went to bed immediately after dinner. I needed a lot of sleep because I had been without a decent night's rest for so long. There was another reason for this. I didn't want to face the loneliness that overcame me with Dongwei still gone, and the unbearable thought of him still at the labor camp. Also, I was deeply anguished because of losing Falun Gong.

Waiting for my beloved was the worst torment I ever suffered. Days turned into nights and nights turned into days. The time passed so slowly.

I was finally allowed to go visit Dongwei at the labor camp. For ordinary prisoners, direct family members can visit once a month. But for Falun Gong practitioners, there was no regular schedule. Family members could only request a visit and wait for a notice from the prison. Some practitioners have not seen family members for years.

It was a long trip by bus. The labor camp was located in a southern suburb of Beijing, which was a long way from downtown. I had to switch buses several times, so I left home early in the morning. It took two or three hours to arrive at the front door of Tuanhe Labor Camp.

I entered the labor camp through a magnificently decorated door. I felt totally out of place and my heart was filled with grief. A place where they locked up good people was decorated like the entrance to a mansion.

After I entered through the gate, I found that the compound was even more impressive than Xin'an Labor Camp, where I had been. I saw flowers and beautifully manicured lawns. I even saw rabbits and deer running through meadows. The guards who were our guides said that all this was to dazzle international organizations and foreign reporters who came to the camp.

We were taken to a room where we waited a long time. Then a guard who seemed to be a higher official came in. He said it was possible some foreign reporters might visit that day, so we had to read a booklet on how we were to respond if one of them spoke to us. It was called *How to Answer Foreign Reporters' 60 Questions*. I browsed through the booklet. I remember the following:

Q: "Are you imprisoned because you practice Falun Gong?"
A: "No. I'm here because I 'disrupted society's rules.' "
Q: "Are inmates ever beaten and abused?"
A: "No."

Since elementary school through graduate school, I had been given many standard responses. I had memorized all of them so that I would pass my exams. But this time I became indignant with the prepared answers. I discarded the booklet somewhere nearby.

The guard continued to give us more responses. "When you respond to foreign reporters, you can't say that people are beaten here, nor can you tell them about the dispatch facilities and intensive units."

A lady of around 40 said, "But last time I came here to meet my husband, he had wounds all over his body!"

The guard looked at her sharply and said, "Whose relative are you? Do you still want to see him or not?"

The lady went silent.

I looked out the window and noticed a small isolated courtyard near the front door of Tuanhe Labor Camp. It looked just like the one I remembered at Xin'an Labor Camp. I suspect it was the Intensive Unit where they held Falun Gong practitioners.

It was clear to me that a foreign reporter would never think that something cruel was going on inside such an ordinary-looking one-story house. The courtyard probably wouldn't attract a reporter's attention either, and the inmates they would be allowed to interview were carefully selected.

When I saw the Intensive Unit out the window, I recalled a chance meeting at a friend's house after I was released. Jun Wu was tortured in the Intensive Unit of Tuanhe Labor Camp, and he shared some of his experiences with me.

Jun Wu, around 30, was a missile research expert. He and his wife were Falun Gong practitioners. They had lived a happy life until the persecution started in 1999. He was imprisoned in the Tuanhe Labor Camp and suffered inhuman torture. He was tied to a bed board around the clock for three months because he refused to renounce his belief.

His entire body was tied to the bed board with a rope, starting with his head and going down his neck, chest, abdomen, hands and feet. He couldn't move. He was kept in a tiny, dark, windowless cell, 2 meters long and 1.5 meters wide. He was forbidden to wash his face, brush his teeth, or relieve himself in the restroom.

Worse still, they would periodically tighten the ropes and beat him, and he was sexually abused at times. A foreign reporter would never be allowed to know about such things.

The guard realized that we were appalled at what he was telling us, so he left, but not before threatening us one last time. I decided to ignore the standard answers. A couple of minutes later, some inmates were brought in. One of them was Dongwei.

I had not seen him for nearly a year. I was shocked by his appearance. His hair was chopped short and I noticed white stubble. He was very thin, and his face was dark and rough.

We stared at each other silently, each of us searching for words. Tears ran down my cheeks. He tried to be strong and comfort me. Instead, tears came quickly, flowing down his cheeks. We held hands tightly, choking and sobbing. Tears clouded my eyes and I couldn't see his face clearly. It was the first time I had ever seen Dongwei cry.

A poem came to my mind, "Spring in the Mansion," by the ancient Chinese poet Ouyang Xiu.

> When drinking our fill, I planned to tell her the day I was leaving.
> Instead of speaking, my beauty sobbed pitifully.

Normally we ask someone, "How are you?" as a greeting, to show we care about them. But I could not ask him this. Didn't I already know how he was doing? Wasn't I just released from a place like this? I was at a loss and there was no way to comfort him. We were only allowed 20 minutes, and I honestly have no idea what we talked about.

Suddenly the guards were shouting orders. They made the inmates stand in a row and march out of the room. Staring at Dongwei's weak body and thin back moving away from me, I finally realized that the visiting time had passed and I was losing him again. Everyone's eyes were red from crying.

———— • ————

In early 2001, before the Chinese New Year, the CCP staged and aired a horrifying piece of propaganda, the infamous "self-immolation" of supposed Falun Gong practitioners.[16]

Many people assumed the program to be an actual news story, which was what the CCP intended. Nowadays, in foreign countries on the Internet, you can see the pictures slowed down and the many errors and oversights pointed out. It's clear that the "news" story was yet another CCP-fabricated vilification of Falun Gong.

But at the time, the images flew by in a flurry of horror, amidst carefully constructed propagandistic narration. I saw this "news" report on CCTV's Topics in Focus news program along with everyone

---

16   Here is a video discussing the hoax: http://www.youtube.com/watch?v=cek-6yplMAE

else. It was terrifying, absolutely horrendous. People setting fire to themselves, victims shouting, police spraying them with fire extinguishers. Violent chills swept down my entire body.

After the incident, I was down for two weeks with a fever and a bad cough. Before, when I was cultivating, I had not needed to go to a hospital or take medicine for anything. If I was uncomfortable, it would be gone immediately after I practiced the exercises. The exercises were far better than taking drugs. But now I wasn't doing the exercises and was struck with illness.

After seeing the show, Dongwei's 75-year-old father shot me a critical look and began interrogating me furiously.

I didn't know yet that it had been faked, and I replied simply, "Cultivators are forbidden to commit suicide."

I stopped there instead of continuing with what I wanted to say: "If it were not forbidden, I would have killed myself in the labor camp, and then you never would have seen me again!"

In fact, Dongwei's mother had practiced Falun Gong before the persecution, and she was cured of high blood pressure that had bothered her for many years. Her knee problem was also much better.

However, after the persecution began, the retired lady came under huge pressure from her workplace. The CCP has a practice of forcing relatives and workplaces to guarantee that a practitioner will not appeal for Falun Gong. Workplace officials have to closely monitor their employees' movements because if a practitioner goes to Beijing to appeal, the workplace will be fined.

Her workplace even threatened her husband, who was not a cultivator. She could not withstand the pressure and gave up. After she stopped practicing, her health problems returned, and now she can no longer walk properly.

CHAPTER TWELVE

At the end of May 2001, Dongwei was released from Tuanhe Labor Camp. Just as I had been, he was taken to the police station before returning home. My parents-in-law were finally reunited with their son, in a heartwarming scene full of grief and joy.

The two elderly people had difficulty expressing themselves, but they showed their love, sadness, and joy by the tears rolling down their faces. My parents cooked a lavish dinner, and we could finally be together as a family.

That night, after our parents had gone to sleep, Dongwei and I went to our room. We sat and stared at each other and sighed, full of emotions. My loving eyes saw that he had aged a lot, yet he still had the innocent look of a child. The white hair on his temples belied the innocent look, and my heart was in deep sorrow. Dongwei kept his hair short for a long time after that. With short hair, the white was less noticeable.

When Dongwei used to travel around China, we often played a little game upon his return. I would ask, "Well? Why did your appearance change in only a few days? I need to test you, to see if you are truly my Dongwei."

Then I would ask him little secret questions that only we knew the answers to, such as my room number at the university, our favorite study rooms, his words when he proposed, and many other things. Through this, we relived in our mind the sweet memories of the past.

The final test question was for him to say my nickname.

Sometimes I would move into the game with a seriousness that implied I would feel really unhappy if he couldn't respond correctly to all my questions. I would look at him anxiously and only find relief when he told me the correct answers.

But that night his appearance really *had* changed, and I dared not play that game. I feared that any joking would hurt him deeply.

We had been married for many years and we knew each other well. He must have known what I was thinking, because he called my nickname softly and looked at me with a naughty smile. I immediately burst out laughing.

I moved toward him, wanting to be in his arms, to feel again his warmth, love, and strength. I had dreamed of him holding me tight in his arms countless times during the past year.

But he quickly stepped backward. "Don't touch me!" he said, his hands stretched out, stopping me.

I was dumbfounded and hurt. "Why?"

He said, "I developed scabies in the labor camp, and I haven't recovered yet."

My heart ached even more strongly and I replied, "I don't care. I just want you to hug me."

Dongwei smiled at me with a familiar expression and said, "Don't be childish. I promise to give you a great hug after I recover."

Scabies is an infectious mite that is common in labor camps. Because prisoners are not allowed to take showers or do laundry, the filthiness is beyond description. I told other team members when I was in the dispatch center, "After coming here, I learned another way a person can die. One can die of the filth in this place."

I don't know who invented such a punishment. It's difficult for people who haven't been in that environment to understand. Those living in such filth can tell you that it's as bad as any other torture method. I knew of many people who had come down with scabies, but it didn't occur to me that Dongwei might have suffered from it.

His scabies was cured after he took daily showers for a while. When I finally received his great hug, I stayed in his arms for a long time. We didn't want to be apart anymore.

Dongwei was severely injured at the dispatch center, but he didn't tell his parents. Sometimes his parents asked about life in the labor camp. He just told them "not bad" and changed to another topic at once. He was even reluctant to talk to me about it.

Once I asked him whether the guards used electric batons to shock him. He only vaguely replied "Brrr," and nothing more. I knew he didn't want me to worry about him, but I told him that I *must* know this and what it felt like. In the end, I got him to tell me, and he said after some thought, "It was not the worst for me, compared to others. It was only one baton. It was like being bitten by a serpent."

I could not hold back my tears, and no longer had the courage to ask for more details. I could imagine the extreme pain from the bite of a serpent. Later, I heard some practitioners talk about being shocked simultaneously with several—even ten or more—electric batons with 100,000-volt charges.

They said it felt like ten thousand arrows penetrating the heart, or ten thousand serpents biting the brain simultaneously. The shocks burned the flesh and caused painful muscle spasms and shortness of breath, or inability to breathe.

Dongwei and I were unable to bring back the carefree and happy life we had before—something blocked my mind. Physical wounds are generally cured after a rest, but mental wounds are more difficult to remove.

Before, we shared everything like close friends, but after the labor camp, there was a barrier in our relationship that didn't let us talk freely with each other. Of course it wasn't because we didn't love each other as much as before, but we had no magic wand to remove the wounds from the torture we suffered in the labor camp. We just couldn't talk about it.

Dongwei was terribly thin, so my mother-in-law took it upon herself to cook delectable meals. He gained half a kilogram every two days. After a month, he had gained almost 20 pounds and was almost the same weight as before. He joked with me that a monkey (his Chinese Zodiac sign) was gaining weight as fast as a pig.

I asked him why he lost 10 kg (22 lb.). He told me that they had to do hard labor. They had to wrap the "sanitary" chopsticks night and day at the dispatch center. At Tuanhe Labor Camp, he also made some kind of export products, but I can't remember what he said they were. Now we finally understood why products that are "Made in China" are so cheap.

———◆———

For a long time after I returned home from the labor camp, my stupefied condition didn't go away.

Dongwei repeatedly brought me to see specialists at the Department of Neurology at a hospital. They firmly informed me I was suffering from depression and asked if I had recently experienced any trauma to my spirit.

Our physical condition improved slowly after we returned home, so our relatives and friends thought we had recovered. In their minds, as long as we had healthy bodies and were without injuries, we had recovered from the ordeal.

It reminded me of a story from a close friend of mine who is also a practitioner. After the persecution of Falun Gong began, her mother, under a policeman's threats, took her to a mental hospital to keep her from being sentenced to a prison term. She was forced to take unknown medicine and receive electroshock therapy.

Her mother told her, "My dear, if you would become insane, I would take care of you for the rest of your life!"

Her mother apparently believed that a healthy physical condition was the fundamental necessity for a human being, and the wellbeing of the spirit was of secondary importance. After more than 50 years of the CCP's cruel and inhuman reign, it seems the Chinese people have given up the luxury of mental health for the more pressing concern of physical safety.

————•————

When I went back to work, I had to learn everything anew. I picked up a stack of English language documents and was astounded. I looked at the letters and it was just like Greek to me. I had lost my English and could recognize only a few words. My job was working in the international finance department—English was a must. If I couldn't read English, I would lose my ability to work.

It took several months for me to become fluent in English again. I registered for an evening English class to help me recall my English vocabulary.

One night, as I opened the door to go to class, a man almost fell into my house.

I was scared for a moment, but then I recognized him. He was a young man from our housing management company, and we knew each other quite well. It took me a moment to realize he had been listening to our private conversation and got caught.

Then I suddenly understood—the police had assigned him to monitor us. I wanted to question him, but then I realized he must have been forced into this situation. So I just pretended not to have seen him, closed the door, and left. After that, I saw him many times outside our home.

Then something unexpected happened. Dongwei started suffering again from gastric intestinal disease, which had been cured when he started practicing Falun Gong. He was again unable to eat fresh or cold food. He was often in pain and broke out in a cold sweat.

At the same time, I found myself suffering too. When I had practiced Falun Gong, no matter how severely the flu hit others around me during the winter season, even those at my office, I did not come down with it. But now I had suffered colds several times.

After practicing Falun Gong, I was not afraid of cold weather. I always felt warmth around my body, and the cold did not affect me. However, in the labor camp I was always freezing and couldn't fall asleep. Now back home, I kept shaking even when I was covered with a quilt and wearing a sweater.

These symptoms remained until we started practicing Falun Gong again.

After having experienced imprisonment in a labor camp, the affection between us improved greatly. We were more secure in our love and had grown closer. I had always loved Dongwei very much, of course, but I spent a lot of time hoping that he could take care of me, wishing he would be more considerate, and wanting him to satisfy my emotional needs. When I felt he wasn't paying enough attention to me, I would sometimes get angry.

After we returned home and I saw his cruelly tortured body, I felt a greater responsibility for our relationship. I became fonder of him and showed it through greater tenderness. I decided secretly in my heart that I must treat him well and take care of him. We must be there for each other, support each other and conquer this hardship together.

In the past, especially before practicing Falun Gong, I used the word "divorce" often, even though I was only bluffing. I often used this word when I tried to force him to do something or when my feelings were hurt. I was acting rashly, trying to get him to see things my way.

Now I swore that I would never, ever say that word again. A couple that had experienced such misery and was reunited again could no longer say hurtful things to each other, such as mentioning divorce or separation, not even as a joke.

As I write this today, Dongwei has again been taken from me. I want to be with him, and I will say it with an ancient Chinese verse:

For life or for death, however separated,
To our beloved person we pledged our word.
We hold each other's hands,
We are to grow old together.

---•---

Not long after Dongwei was released from the labor camp, he decided to quit his job. It was not to get a better job, but to reduce the trouble his workplace was experiencing because he had practiced Falun Gong.

Dongwei's colleagues had tried to help him while he was imprisoned. For this, they suffered many hardships after they negotiated with the police.

Not long after we were arrested, Dongwei's workplace invited officials from the Beijing Public Security Bureau to dinner. They thought that simply writing a letter wasn't a big deal and that Dongwei would be released quickly, maybe within one or two days.

The Public Security officials told them during the dinner that Dongwei's case was not a small deal, saying that he had participated in the "Fragrant Hills Meeting" (the Fragrant Hills are northwest of Beijing). The officials took out a photo and showed it to them for a second. No one could make out anything on the photo.

Dongwei's colleagues thought the "Fragrant Hills Meeting" was some major, horrendous crime and they were all frightened. No one dared to ask for Dongwei's release. They simply asked the Public Security Bureau to treat him well and not beat him up.

Only after Dongwei was released did his colleagues have a chance to ask, "What was the Fragrant Hills Meeting that you participated in?" At that point, we all realized how the police thugs had lied. We had lived in Beijing for many years, but Dongwei had never even gone to the Fragrant Hills, much less to any meeting there.

Later, when Dongwei's colleagues went to the dispatch center, they were lied to again. Instead of getting Dongwei released earlier, the dispatch center kept him for an even longer period of time, after realizing the company was wealthy. Officials like to tell wealthy companies that large bribes will help get their employees out sooner or allow them to be treated better.

Still, Dongwei was grateful to his colleagues and decided that he would work even harder for the company after he returned to work.

But now the Internal Security Section (dedicated to Falun Gong persecution) of the Beijing Public Security Bureau often came to Dongwei's workplace to harass them, with the excuse that they needed to "understand Dongwei's thoughts." Every time they came, the company had to send someone to accompany them, treat them to dinner, and so on.

Dongwei felt guilty for bringing these troubles to his company, and decided to resign from his job.

After much discussion, we decided to return to school. Because of the type of work Dongwei had done over the past years, he decided to get an MBA. Applying for a Master of Business Administration required the TOEFL and GMAT tests, so he began to prepare for them.

After returning home from the labor camp, Dongwei also felt that his mind was not as sharp as before. It seemed he could no longer remember things as well. He used to be quite fluent in English. Yet after preparing for quite some time, the test results were still below our expectations.

All the top MBA schools are in the United States. It would not be easy to apply for top U.S. schools with his current test results. In the end, he decided to go to the best MBA school in Asia, the Hong Kong University of Science & Technology.

I decided to enter law school at Peking University and was aiming for another master's degree. I had always wanted to study at Peking University. Dongwei supported me because he had always felt that fate had brought me to Wuhan University because of him.

We had some savings that Dongwei could use for getting his MBA, while I continued to work at my job and took classes in the evenings and on weekends.

It was difficult to study and work at the same time. However, without Dongwei beside me, studying was my way of filling the empty spot in my life. It did its job and I was not lonely. Dongwei's MBA program was intensive, but he often squeezed in some time to come back to Beijing to be with me.

When I first started cultivation in Falun Gong, I thought I would never have to worry too much about laws, because the standards for a cultivator are stricter than the laws.

But now in today's China, Falun Gong practitioners are being punished in the name of law and taken to prisons and labor camps in the name of law.

I decided to understand everything that was happening to Falun Gong and its practitioners from the perspective of the law.

I've always done well in my studies. In high school, I was always at the top of my class, and I had taken the National Matriculation Examination (NME) a year early.

When I entered Wuhan University after high school, I suddenly had quite a lot of competition from other students—I was no longer at the top of the class. But even though most of the time my thoughts centered around dating and relationships, and I didn't study as hard, I was granted scholarships for all four years at the University.

This time, most of my friends thought I wasn't that serious about studying law at Peking University, because most people who pursue a master's degree are doing it to get a promotion at their jobs. Even the professors at the law school said that it was easy to achieve the 70th or 80th percentile, but it would require a great deal of unique interpretation and independent analysis to achieve the 90th percentile.

Before, I hadn't applied myself very hard toward studying for a degree. But this time, I was truly trying to understand the heart of the matter instead of just theory. I was trying to understand the issue of personal freedom, rights, and especially the freedom of belief, on behalf of the hundred million people who practiced Falun Gong. I wanted to find out how the painful near-death ordeal I had been through could be explained in terms of law. So I maintained great strength and vigor during those three years of study, and I achieved the 90th percentile.

Not long after entering law school, I found something strange. There had never been any reference to Falun Gong in any of the laws of the People's Republic of China. The PRC never had any legal or judicial documents citing Falun Gong as illegal or as a "cult."

Neither the Constitution nor the Criminal Law of China mentioned, interpreted, or discussed Falun Gong, or issued an edict that it was a cult. As of today, the Supreme People's Procuratorate has never filed an indictment against Falun Gong, and the Supreme People's Court has not held trials of Falun Gong practitioners according to the Criminal Procedural Laws of China.

The only "evidence" to support Falun Gong being a cult was former Party leader Jiang Zemin's declaration that it was a cult, during an interview with a French reporter from Le Figaro.

Article 80 of the Constitution of the People's Republic of China states, "The President of the People's Republic of China, in pursuance of the decisions by the National People's Congress and its Standing Committee ... issues orders of special pardons; proclaims martial law; proclaims a state of war; and issues mobilization orders."

In other words, declaring anything without a decision by the National People's Congress and its Standing Committee is in violation of the Constitution. Therefore, there are no grounds for law enforcement on the Falun Gong issue.

If a hundred million people were to be named part of a "cult organization," the Supreme People's Courts and Supreme People's Procuratorate would have to enforce a new series of judicial procedures.

On July 20, 1999, the Ministry of Civil Affairs and the Public Security Bureau issued notices banning the practice of Falun Gong. Since both are executive branch agencies, their notices cannot be construed as legal grounds for criminalizing Falun Gong. In fact, these notices are, in themselves, illegal. In addition, according to the spirit of law, laws can only judge one's actions, not one's thoughts.

Therefore, the thousands of "transformation" methods used on Falun Gong practitioners in labor camps are illegal—every single one of them.

This finding shocked me deeply. There is an inherent understanding about laws—they are to be used for righteous means, to promote justice and deter people from wrongdoing. Yet in mainland China, the law has been warped so badly that it is now being manipulated by evil to destroy the good.

During the first days of the persecution, everyone was bombarded with solemn terms such as "banned" and "outlawed." In this petrifying environment, everyone felt a sense of danger and moved to protect themselves. No one could afford the time or effort to consider whether the Chinese Communist Party had the legal right to do what it was doing.

Even today, there are still some people who think Falun Gong practitioners deserve what they get. Beatings are illegal, except against Falun Gong practitioners. Burglary is illegal, except when burglarizing Falun Gong practitioners' houses. The thought is that Falun Gong practitioners are choosing to practice in spite of the ban—they are asking for it. The continuous assault by China's media throughout China has, for all practical purposes, "legalized" any crimes committed against Falun Gong.

In class, we sometimes talked about the issue of Falun Gong. Some professors were sympathetic, but others seemed to have developed the same illogical rationale spewed by the Party's official channels. For instance, a professor on procedural law commented on how the "re-education through labor" system is illegal because it is applying punishment outside the law. Yet, he said, in order to persecute Falun Gong, it is necessary to keep it for a while.

I was utterly stunned by his words. Such logic totally deviated from what a professor of law should believe and teach.

The Chinese legal system no longer adheres to the law. It is just like what the CCP put forth over and over regarding the Tiananmen Square massacre on June 4, 1989: Massacring the students was done because the student leaders had "political ambitions." Because of that, they have to bear the responsibility for the massacre, while those ordering machine guns to be fired on a group of unarmed students are blameless.

Or when peasants' annual salaries are withheld or delayed by the local government, they are going to the extreme by asking for their pay. It's labeled as "threatening the government" and is punished by law, while those refusing to pay the salaries are blameless.

CHAPTER THIRTEEN

In early 2003, colleagues began passing secret messages to each other. "Don't go to Guangzhou on work errands. There is a rapid spread of a lethal epidemic."

About one or two months later, the atmosphere worsened progressively. It was rumored that the so-called "SARS" (severe acute respiratory syndrome) was brought back to Beijing by people who had come from Guangzhou on work errands.

Some claimed that entire hospitals were overflowing with people suffering from the disease. I was puzzled. Why didn't I see any news or reports on this? Isn't it true that the best way to prevent an epidemic from spreading is to publicize the facts and tell people how to protect themselves?

Dongwei's school closed because of SARS, and the students were sent home for two months.

In late March, all governmental agencies in Beijing went on shifts. My workplace was divided into three shifts. It was said that this would help prevent epidemics from breaking out in an entire company should anyone become infected.

Besides going to work or shopping for groceries, I seldom left home. Beijing was like a dead town. The streets were empty, and cars had almost disappeared from the roads.

Once when I was crossing an overpass on my way home from the supermarket, I saw a lady struggling to carry some shopping bags up the stairs. She looked really overburdened, so I offered to help her.

After I helped her onto a public transport bus, she said, "Thank you, I'm very grateful. Nowadays, no one dares to even talk to one another for fear of being infected with SARS. It's rare that anyone offers to help me. Aren't you afraid?"

I shook my head.

"You're not afraid of SARS? Do you practice Falun Gong? I heard that Falun Gong practitioners are very healthy and are not afraid of catching anything."

I had not yet begun cultivating again, and that incident made me stop and think.

Not long after that, I took a taxi home from work, and the taxi driver told me a story that also challenged my thoughts.

One day, while the taxi driver was waiting for customers at the Beijing Train Station, a man asked for a ride. The man was carrying a huge load of village-style bags, and he wanted to go to Fangzhuang, a neighborhood southeast of Beijing.

The driver told me, "I thought because of all the bags that he was just a country hick, and I decided to con him. It generally costs about 15 yuan for a ride to Fangzhuang, but after the man got into the cab, I told him, 'I'm not going to use the meter. I'll charge you 25 yuan. It's the best deal you'll ever get.'"

The man thought it over and agreed. When they were nearing Fangzhuang, the man made a call on his cell phone. "Hi, sweetheart. I'll be home in a few minutes. Can you come down and help me carry all this stuff up? The elders wouldn't let me go without giving me this huge bunch of gifts."

The driver was shocked. This man was a local! If he were to report him, the driver would be in deep trouble. He hurriedly told the man, "Sorry, my brother, I didn't realize you were a local. Just give me 15 yuan. That's enough. I don't dare to take more."

The man grinned, but still handed the driver 25 yuan, saying, "Here. Take it. Maybe I'm repaying a debt from a previous life."

The driver asked, "A previous life? How many Chinese people still believe in such things? What's your faith?"

The passenger responded, "I practice Falun Gong."

After that, the driver told other passengers the story. He said, "If everyone practiced Falun Gong, the entire world would live in peace. I wouldn't try to con people anymore."

By early April, the SARS situation in Beijing had become tense. Most people knew of some friends, colleagues or family members who had been infected with it, and the pressure of SARS on each person's life was mounting.

Yet one day in April, the former Minister of Health, Zhang Wenkang, declared on CCTV's "Topics in Focus" that it was absolutely safe for foreigners and other people to travel to Beijing for work and tourism.

An old friend of Dongwei's and mine from our Wuhan University days came to visit us while Dongwei was home from school. The friend, who happened to work at CCTV, was watching the program with us.

Seeing the alarmed look on my face, he mocked me. "Oh, please, my dear princess, can you not act so surprised—again? I really don't get it, you know. Before, I used to call you childish because you were so simple and innocent. You didn't know of the evil things in this world. But now that you've suffered in a labor camp, I'd think that would be enough to make you grow up. So how come you're still naïve?"

I replied glumly, "In the past, I only watched 'Topics in Focus' on CCTV because I felt that was the only program that dared to speak the truth. But now—"

"You know," he interrupted, "even my economics program is strictly regulated. You can't imagine how much these news programs are controlled. They're simply mouthpieces for the Party. Remember when I visited you right after you were released from the labor camp? Remember the self-immolation incident by Falun Gong practitioners shown on 'Topics in Focus'?"

Of course I remembered.

"Well, as a reporter, I'm very familiar with self-immolation incidents—and they happen suddenly. It's impossible to obtain such quick and comprehensive footage of an incident like that. Especially because it happened in Tiananmen Square.

"Notice all those near-focus, far-focus, portrait, and other camera shots they got of the incident. Those cameras had to have all been set up and ready to shoot. If something happened on the spur of the moment, what reporter could possibly bring all of this equipment to the location so quickly? Also, it takes a while for policemen to find fire extinguishers and get them working. But those people were sprayed with dozens of fire extinguishers immediately after they set themselves on fire. Where did all those things come from?"

I was holding my breath. "You're saying that the entire self-immolation incident was a scam?"

He scoffed. "I can hardly stand your naïveté. You always look so shocked whenever you see something untrue on TV. Every Chinese person in mainland China knows that, except for the date and time, nothing on the news is real."

———•———

The fraud perpetrated in today's China is beyond imagination. Everything goes, from fake cigarettes, beer, wine, and sausages, to poisonous rice, oil, and milk powder. Every day, more items are added to the list of poisonous food on the China Food website.

I remember a blogger once wrote, "Breathing polluted air, eating fake or poisonous food, drinking sewer-quality water, yet still having to protect oneself from other people's schemes, watching the rising price of meat, worrying about stocks collapsing, checking the anti-burglar door several times a day—even trying to remember the winning lottery numbers from one's dreams—living in mainland China is just too tiring. Not physically, but from the deepest, most minute part of one's soul."

In fact, changes in the environment or the food are not the most frightening. The most frightening changes are the ones in people's hearts.

Nowadays, some people have accepted some of the ugliest and most morally depraved phenomena in society, and even actively find reasons to support and explain these phenomena.

For example, everyone knows that almost all higher-ranking officials in China are corrupt and lustful, but most people think that's just the way it is. Some even say that if they had that many enticements, be it wealth or women, they would also be like that.

I often found myself lamenting, "The entire society is ill, both physically and mentally. People are bad to the core."

In modern life, even someone who knows what is righteous and good is easily influenced by the environment and his or her own desires. Human hearts are often complicated and easily swayed.

Yet, for someone who knows the universal principles of Truthfulness, Compassion, and Tolerance, how can she be willing to ride downstream with society?

The famous Chinese historical character Qu Yuan, who lived

around 300 B.C., in the Warring States Period, wrote the following words in the poem, "The Fisherman":

> *I have heard that someone who has just washed his hair will definitely clear dust off his hat, and someone who has just bathed his body will definitely shake the dirt from his clothes. How can one bear to have his clean and pure body be polluted by worldly dirt again? I would rather jump into the Xiang River, and die in the stomachs of fish at the bottom of the river, than to let my pure nature be buried under the world's dirt.*

———•———

When SARS was taking its toll across Beijing, I rarely left my home, so I finally found some time to indulge in reading. I especially read works by the Soviet writer Aleksandr Isayevich Solzhenitsyn.

Solzhenitsyn was sentenced to eight years of "re-education through labor" and charged with engaging in anti-Soviet propaganda and secretly establishing anti-Soviet organizations. All for criticizing Stalin in a letter to a friend. After his release, he was exiled to Kazakhstan, where he wrote many novels exposing the atrocities in Soviet prisons and labor camps. I was deeply touched by his remark that "time offers no redemption."

Indeed, a person doesn't necessarily gain wisdom or improve his or her morality with increasing age. Aren't there dozens of the older generation among us? Yet as I see it, so many in China do not display the least bit of wisdom that should come with their age. Then there are those who have turned completely selfish after having survived too many political campaigns in China. Nothing has brought great happiness and enjoyment to the Chinese people.

Money, the root of the world's striving, does not offer liberation from misery, either. Nor can one reach a high spiritual realm simply by being philanthropic. Giving money to those who have none because one has a surplus doesn't really do much to change the inner self. Worse are those who become greedier the more wealth they accumulate. One only needs to observe China's dishonest officials and their corrupt deeds to understand.

Neither does knowledge offer redemption if one does not improve one's character. Today there are many people who are highly accomplished and educated, but their educational attainment doesn't kindle a sense of responsibility, and they do not follow the proverb,

"The educated are the conscience of society." In fact, they simply use their advanced degrees to earn more money and live a better life. There are some whose compassion has dwindled to nothing. They instead develop greater apathy or antipathy toward the weak and unprivileged.

Once, a classmate told me of his "greatest ambition." He had already bought two houses, one in Beijing and one in Shanghai, and his ambition was to buy a third, which he was getting ready to do.

I mentioned to him the many people who do not even own one house or could not afford to buy enough food. I reminded him of the countless Henan residents who had contracted HIV after trying to sell blood. "Who would sell blood if they had the money to buy food?" I asked him.

He muttered, "Sure, sure, of course," and then continued to talk about his third house. He used to be spirited and energetic. Now he seemed to be inflated from the riches he'd been enjoying.

Remembering this, I became a little sad. What can make someone change like that? For thousands of years, the Chinese taught virtues such as benevolence, justice, courtesy, wisdom, and trust. There are stories of heroes and heroines of old who gave up their lives to protect these virtues. And what about the splendid dynasties where strong morals were the basis for all actions by the wealthy? How did such great Chinese heritage go astray and turn into today's "more civilized and advanced" society?

Solzhenitsyn's criticisms of the Soviet Union were not focused on political crimes, but on moral ones. The ruling Communist Party forcibly converted everyone to atheism. People who believe in nothing have no moral yardstick and are easily pulled into committing wrongdoing.

———◆———

It came time to choose a thesis for my law degree, and I discussed the matter with my advisor. I told him that I wanted to write on the issue of human rights abuses against particular groups in society.

He paused for a while and replied, "I'm not saying you can't do it, but you have the burden of proof. Which particular group do you have in mind? Peasant workers? Women? Children?"

I said, "Falun Gong."

The advisor immediately went pale. "You can't write about Falun Gong!"

"Why not?" I asked.

He told me anxiously, "If you knew what had happened to the professor who argued against the Tiananmen Massacre, you would not be asking why!"

He was persistent, and in the end, I changed my mind and wrote about bank regulation reform. After all, I spent three years at the university, and I still wanted to get my degree.

During the defense of my thesis, I realized that most theses are not creative, but cut and dried, including mine. I did not see any sense in the motto, "Encompassing and Forbearing Everything, Encouraging Freedom of Thought" as espoused by the previous Peking University President, Cai Yuanpei. There was no freedom of thought here.

The only thesis that aroused a little of my interest was by a girl who wrote on the issue of appealing when faced with unjust laws. Her argument was that it was better not to appeal, because 80 to 90 percent of the time it was bound to fail, and would actually cause further harm to oneself. Therefore, the entire Law of Appeals should be abolished. Yes, that was a very creative thesis. It shows the kind of resignation people feel in such a corrupt system.

My defense of the bank regulations reform passed successfully, and I obtained my Master of Law in June 2004. Yet I didn't know how this hard-earned degree would help me with what I had hoped to learn.

My efforts to understand the law turned out to be just an intermediate step in finally discovering the truth about the CCP, and my studies only enlightened me on the subject to a certain extent. I knew now that the persecution had been entirely illegal, and that the CCP dared to go against the law, to be above the law.

But I didn't fully understand why Falun Gong had been persecuted, and just how deep the monstrosity of the CCP went, until I read the *Nine Commentaries on the Communist Party*. Most Chinese people don't really understand how inherently evil the CCP is until after they have read the *Nine Commentaries*. Even after I survived the labor camp, I didn't really understand the full situation, because the Party itself had always controlled my education, and it didn't want me to know.

———•———

Two years after he started the program, Dongwei completed his MBA, returned to Beijing, and began looking for work. He finally decided on a full-time position with an American nonprofit organization, the Asia Foundation, in their Beijing office. He provided peasant workers with legal assistance and consultation. He had always wanted to do some kind of humanitarian work. In China, delaying peasant workers' pay is commonplace, and the peasant workers have no idea how to protect their rights under existing laws.

Dongwei deeply sympathized with them and was engrossed in his work. Many of our discussions focused on these peasant workers. He had similar feelings about them as he did for those children we once helped through Project Hope. He would often donate books or clothing to a peasant workers' training school in Beijing, which was built by the peasant workers themselves.

———•———

Two of the most commonly seen words in Beijing are "Obtain Certification." These two words hang on walls and bridges and are written on floors. Wherever you go, you can't miss these words. A cell phone number is written next to them. What does it mean? It means you should give a call and if you have enough cash on hand, you can obtain fake degrees, fake driver licenses, fake education certificates, and other fake documentation, even fake wedding certificates. I'm still unclear on the purpose of a fake wedding certificate.

One day after work, I complained to Dongwei, "Today, someone told me that there is no use in having so many master's degrees, it still does not compare to a doctorate."

To make me happy, Dongwei said, "Who said that? He must be a doctorate holder himself. In today's world, interdisciplinary knowledge is the key. Two master's degrees are far better!"

Despite my husband's kind words, I still felt that having a doctorate was the epitome of wisdom. The doctorate title even appears in your name's prefix. If the president of a nation also has a doctorate, he could be called "Dr. XX" instead of "President XX." Therefore, I thought that if my grades were so good at Peking University, it should be no problem to get a doctorate, right?

Recalling that my master's advisor wouldn't let me write my thesis about Falun Gong, I decided it would be difficult to get him to agree on a Ph.D. thesis. So I decided to find another advisor.

I approached a fairly well-known Ph.D. advisor—one who was more straightforward. After hearing about my desire to get a doctorate, he came right to the point. "In China today, most people get a Ph.D. in order to find a good job. People such as you who already have a good job and want to obtain a Ph.D. . . . hmm, is that to aggrandize yourself? To climb up further, right? Well, it's true that the nation is trying to promote younger people to become leaders and officials, and to have more education. All right, no problem. I can help you, but you've got to tell me what's in it for me."

I didn't know what to say. Seeing my shock, he explained further. "For example, if some bureau chief or minister wants to study a Ph.D. under me, and I accept him, it would then be much easier for me to find some confidential documents for my research, or to travel somewhere, wouldn't it?"

Now I understood where this was going. But as a financial analyst, I didn't have anything to offer. It looked like my Ph.D. dream had just gone down the drain.

I said, "Bureau chiefs and ministers are all so busy. Where would they find the time to write a thesis?"

He laughed. "He doesn't need to write it himself—his secretary can do it."

————◆————

In 1998, the Chairman of the National People's Congress, Qiao Shi, ordered a thorough study of Falun Gong. He concluded, "Falun Gong brings hundreds of benefits and not a single harm to the nation and its people."

In fact, before 1999, national media reported on the miraculous health benefits, both physical and mental, that Falun Gong brought to its practitioners. That's one reason there had been so many practitioners at my workplace.

After the onset of the persecution, during my company's health checks, many of my young colleagues were again found to suffer the "Three Highs"—high cholesterol, high blood pressure, and high blood sugar.

When I returned from the labor camp, the carefree and confident me no longer existed. I doubted myself and wondered what I had done wrong. I was often overcome with sorrow. I would become unbalanced by any little disturbance.

I read many books that taught how to change one's mental state, but none were effective. I couldn't even behave foolishly for fun. Yet whenever I remembered Mr. Li Hongzhi's teachings, I would be instantly filled with the kind of compassion and strength I experienced when I was cultivating. Any grievances or unhappiness vanished.

Mr. Li taught that the Buddha Fa[17] is not an ordinary theory, but that there are infinitely deeper meanings within it. It slowly sank in—the idea of cultivating without studying the Fa or practicing the exercises was a lie. If there is no Fa to guide one's cultivation, how can one cultivate? If society's norms were able to guide one's cultivation and maintain morality in society, the world would not have sunk to the level it has.

Whenever I reasoned it out in my mind, the lies I heard in the labor camp disintegrated. Reflecting on my experience as a cultivator of Falun Gong made me certain, more than ever before, that character improvement obtained through cultivating Falun Dafa was genuine. Dafa brings hope for people to be saved from human suffering and

17 Fa—can be translated as "Law," "Way," or "Dharma." At the highest level, Buddha Law encompasses the characteristic of the universe, Truthfulness-Compassion-Tolerance.

to improve their spiritual character.

The degree of corruption, deception, and moral depravation has reached an astounding level in modern Chinese society. Correspondingly, it has brought problems of environmental degradation, climate change, air, water, and food pollution, and countless "natural" disasters. Humans are destroying that which sustains them.

My cultivating would not just be for me, but for the nation, for others. Cultivating in a righteous practice is beneficial to the nation and its people.

Some friends realized I was thinking about cultivating again and became nervous. Some of them advised me to cultivate in Buddhism instead.

In fact, the first time I read a Buddhist text in college, years ago, I was deeply attracted to it. Sakyamuni (the historical Buddha, Guatama Siddhartha) had teachings on reincarnation, retribution, and rewards that became an integral part of my outlook on life. I loved reading Sakyamuni's stories, and I remember many of them.

Sakyamuni also repeated many times that his teachings would only offer salvation for five hundred years after he reached nirvana. He said that after two thousand years it would be the end of the Dharma-Ending Period. During that time, even monks in monasteries would have difficulty saving themselves because they would not be able to understand the true meaning of the Buddha Fa.

Sakyamuni talked about "Past Buddha, current Buddha, future Buddha." I remember when I read this, I wanted to find the "Future Buddha." Sakyamuni also talked about the "Holy King Who Turns the Wheel," and he said that the Holy King Who Turns the Wheel would descend to the human world to teach his Dharma during the end of the Dharma-Ending Period.

Maybe that's why Falun Dafa has spread so quickly, not just throughout China, but also to over eighty other countries within 15 years.

———— • ————

One night, Teacher asked me in a dream if I still wanted to cultivate. I answered, "Yes, I've always wanted to!" I burst into tears. When I woke up, my face was drowned in tears, and I was muttering, "Teacher, I am very sincere!"

The process of regaining my soul was a painful one. It was like rebirth after death, but it was also like rebuilding myself once again.

The previous me had not been mature enough to face the storm. I had no resistance in the face of lies and brutality. This time, I felt a strong, determined quality developing inside me.

Charles De Gaulle once said, "Hardship attracts the brave and strong, for only when they embrace hardships can they truly recognize themselves." Truly surpassing hardships and pain in my life, I believed a mature mind would become my greatest source of strength.

I felt that my faith in Truthfulness, Compassion, and Tolerance had grown diamond-strong. Never again would it waver.

I returned to my cultivation path in the spring of 2003, and Dongwei started cultivating again, too.

We were still under surveillance, and we were very much afraid of being arrested again. Whenever I practiced the exercises at home, I had to pull down the shades and keep the stereo at its lowest setting. I had to hide my books in a safe place after I finished reading in order to be ready for any sudden inspection. We were under great mental pressure every day.

After I started cultivation, my body and mind were cleansed again. It didn't take long for my body to recover from the brutal torture I had suffered in the labor camp. Dongwei also recovered physically, and his hair turned black again.

CHAPTER FOURTEEN

When I was studying for my Master of Law degree at Peking University, Dongwei often joked, "You're going to create a lot of pressure for me. Won't it be embarrassing when other people find out my wife has one more degree than I do?"

And I would say, "I heard that an MBA is equivalent to two master's degrees, so we're still on par."

However, when I wanted to go to Cambridge for my third master's degree, Dongwei began to really feel the pressure. "If you get a third master's, I'll have no hope of being on par with you. Unless I get a doctorate, everyone will think I'm afraid of my wife."

Nevertheless, in early 2004, I began to apply to study overseas. I would return after completing my studies. I wanted to get away from China and learn for myself what it meant to live abroad. I reasoned that the information blockade in mainland China had risen to unprecedented heights, and it was difficult to discover the truth on any issue while still in China.

I had always wanted to go to England because I liked to read classical English literature novels, which filled me with a sense of longing. America gave me the impression of a metropolis with skyscrapers and tall buildings, but England gave me a totally different picture—a big, broad piece of grassland with a huge rubber tree in the center, with its leaves and branches extending out like an umbrella.

I imagined taking my favorite book and sitting below the canopy.

This dream became a reality many times while I was in England, for almost every college at Cambridge University has such a classic place.

In March, I was accepted into Cambridge and began preparing to go to England. However, in June, I came down with some strange health symptoms. I suspected I might be pregnant.

Now that I had been accepted into Cambridge University, I wasn't sure if I should be elated or upset. Dongwei and I really loved children, and it hadn't been easy to wait this long. But were we really cut out to be parents? It was scary! What if we failed at being good parents?

Without telling Dongwei, I went to the hospital for a pregnancy test. A 40-year-old female doctor told me, "You're pregnant! Do you want the child?"

I looked at her, shocked. "Do I want it?"

The doctor was a little impatient. "What's the matter with you? Do you want the child? You have two choices—go to the second floor to get a pregnancy exam if you want the child, or if you don't want it, go to the third floor for an abortion."

I was stunned. A cultivator is forbidden to kill, especially a human being. Yet this doctor talked about it so nonchalantly. I recalled that in movies I'd seen, the doctor congratulated the pregnant woman with a wonderful smile on his or her face. Having or not having the child had never crossed my mind.

Seeing my stunned expression, she raised her voice. "Are you an idiot? Don't you even know if you want your child?"

I replied hurriedly, "Yes, I want to have the child!"

She gave me instructions to get the pregnancy exam and hurried out the door. "Next!"

After China's so-called medical reform, almost everyone was suddenly without medical insurance. People couldn't afford to see a doctor. Unless death is imminent, most people simply won't go to a hospital. However, even with this reduction in patients, there is still a shortage of hospitals in China. They are very crowded, and the clinic I went to was no exception. Rooms and corridors were packed with people.

I had to fight my way to the second floor. Seeing all the sick people made me a little depressed. Humans really do live with hardship, I thought. I also sympathized with the doctor, despite her rude attitude. It would be really hard to keep a happy face while seeing so many sick people all day long.

I remembered that pregnant women should keep a happy countenance, so I tried to entertain myself by recalling some funny things I had heard.

The Evolution of Mom's Clothes:
  1st baby: You begin wearing maternity clothes as soon as
    your OB/GYN confirms your pregnancy.
  2nd baby: You wear your regular clothes for as long as possible.
  3rd baby: Your maternity clothes are your regular clothes.

I had to wait for quite some time before it was my turn. I was told I would be given a lot of tests—for hepatitis, brain diseases, STDs, AIDS, etc.

"Is this necessary?" I asked. "Can I opt out on any of these tests?"

"It's your choice. But if you want to give birth in this hospital you have to take them."

I had to wait again to have my blood drawn. I was handed seven or eight tubes to be filled with blood. I was shocked. "Seven or eight tubes? What on earth for?"

The nurse was very patient, a relief after the rudeness of the doctor. "The blood will be sent to different labs," she explained, "as not all tests can be done in the same lab. Therefore, we need multiple samples."

"I'm pregnant. Is it safe to take so much blood?"

She smiled. "Each tube only takes about 5 ml of blood. So it won't add up to more than 50 ml." Then perhaps she realized this didn't sound right, for 50 ml is a fair amount of blood. She said, "That's true, when I gave birth I didn't have to have so many tests. No one had heard of AIDS back then."

On my way home, I silently told the little life in my belly, "Baby, don't be afraid of being born into the dangers in this human society. Don't be afraid of life, sickness, and death. You are being born out of your own choice. Your mom and dad will try to give you the best environment we can!"

I'm not sure I would have promised all that if I'd known that both her parents would be taken from her before she reached her second birthday.

When Dongwei got home from work that day, I told him the news. Unexpectedly, he was filled with joy! Looking back, I guess he had just been respecting my opinion when he agreed not to have a child. It definitely wasn't his idea. If I was honest with myself, I had to admit, "Why would I not love kids?" When the persecution started, in the face of a horrifying reality, I had made the decision to wait.

I decided to be happy.

I immediately wrote to Cambridge and asked for a one-year extension before starting school. The Cambridge staff had no objections after hearing that I was pregnant and said there would be no problem with coming the following year.

———— • ————

I've heard that older parents tend to pamper their children. I was 34 when I found out I was pregnant, and I was certainly one of those parents from day one. As the baby grew inside me, I felt deep motherly love. I knew I would give everything for this baby. I took advice from all the nutrition books at my disposal. I followed all the instructions in books for pregnant ladies. Oh my, did I gain weight! But I didn't care. Dongwei used to be about 40 pounds heavier than I. But in the last month I weighed more than he did!

He couldn't help but notice my affection for the baby, and once he joked, "I used to think that you loved me 100 percent. But compared to the baby, I think it is now something like 70 percent." He didn't seem to notice that he loved the baby just as much as I did.

Dongwei used to act like an overgrown child, but after he found out about the baby, he quickly changed and talked and acted more like a father. I never thought a father would love his child so much. He reported his daily activities to his unborn baby, and I thought he spoke to her more than to me.

In the past, he would often reject my requests to recite poems or other activities because he thought that sort of thing was too girlish. But now when I said it was for the baby, he no longer refused anything I asked.

Every night we would recite Teacher's *Hong Yin* poems. We hoped that she was a baby who would accept the principles of Truthfulness, Compassion, and Tolerance while still in the womb! Every time we recited the poems, she responded. She must really have liked them!

She was very active, always moving around like a fish swimming in water. I remember that whenever I thought about the persecution of Falun Gong and became depressed, tears would run down my cheeks uncontrollably, and she would start kicking hard in my belly.

All four grandparents were thrilled that I was pregnant, but they were also worried that having a baby when I was over 30 might be dangerous for me. However, because I practiced Falun Gong, my body was in excellent shape. It was a healthy pregnancy, with few or no complaints. Up to the night of the birth, I was still meditating and practicing the exercises. The bulging belly didn't stop me.

Right away our daughter showed her tendency for being on time. She arrived on the exact day the doctor predicted, and we spent a happy, nervous, blissful, and busy time together.

The following was translated into English from Dongwei's blog to introduce the first year of our baby.

Tiantian's First Year

It will be four more days to the Year of the Dog. Our little "monkey" is turning one.

Name: Tiantian[18]
Date of birth:
Jan. 25, 2005 20:26 hours
Height/wt: 54.5cm, 3.85kg

2 weeks: Developed some small pimples on the face. Her mother looked at her and whispered, "Which family does this ugly girl belong to?" We applied lotion and gave her some homemade carrot-apple juice. The pimples disappeared within three weeks.

1 month: Sleeps at 9 p.m. and gets up 6 hours later. Lets mom and dad sleep through the night.

2 months: Raises her head.

---

18 Tian in Chinese can mean sky or heaven.

3 months: Went to the park with us for the first time on her 100th day, and we took some outdoor pictures.

4 months: Turns over from her side and nudges forward.

5 months: Learns to crawl.

6 months: An experienced crawler already. Is waving "good-bye." She really waves.

7 months: Sits already without falling over.

8 months: Calls for her "mom." Problem—she calls everyone she meets "Mom." Stood up by the bed once, holding onto the side of the bed. Develops a strong desire to learn to walk. Can stagger a few steps.

9 months: Calls for "Dad," but only when Dad is not around.

10 months: Always wants to be with the company when someone is visiting.

11 months: Learns to walk. Recognizes 50 pictures.

12 months: 10 kg, 74cm. Walks by holding onto walls and beds for support. Still a little wobbly on her feet. Can say her own surname, and says the words "mom, dad, grandpa, aunt, hold milk, cat," and many more. When asked about her age, she lifts her first finger, but sometimes she raises all five fingers.

———•———

Seven months after Tiantian's birth, I began to pack for Cambridge University in England to obtain my Master of Finance degree.

I knew it might be difficult for me to get out of China, since the state was closely monitoring me. I already had a passport from before, which had not yet expired. I didn't tell anyone except family and close friends that I was preparing to go abroad. When I spoke to them on the phone, no one dared to even mention the trip, nor could we say goodbye over the phone. At the airport, my family was also in a state of heightened stress. They reminded me again and again to call them immediately after I got through all the boarding procedures. They waited at the airport for my call and didn't leave until afterward. None of us would have been surprised if I had been discovered by police and prevented from boarding.

———•———

Cambridge is an elegant and beautiful small town with a rich cultural atmosphere and about 100,000 residents.

The River Cam meanders through the center of town, with flowers and willows dotting the banks. It is a tradition in Cambridge to push oneself with a pole on a boat down the river.

I found the entire campus filled with lush greenery and a scholarly flavor, looking like a dream castle. Besides students and residents, tourists flooded the campus daily. Yet surprisingly, no matter how packed the place might get, the entire campus never lost its tranquility. The thick cultural atmosphere in Cambridge was utterly mysterious.

My college, Hughes Hall, was not large, but it was comfortable and relaxing. I was assigned to a two-story house with three other students. There was an American guy studying law, an American girl studying archaeology, and an Indian studying economics.

Mixing students from different backgrounds and programs is characteristic of Cambridge, so as to allow interdisciplinary interaction, communication, and inspiration.

I lived in a small room upstairs. Outside my window there was a beautiful tree. I don't know what kind of tree it was, but whenever I called Dongwei on the phone, there would be birds in the tree chirping at me. The birds were not afraid of people at all. Sometimes when I opened the window, instead of flying away, they would pop their heads up and look at me.

Cambridge has educated many famous people throughout history, including some who have revolutionized the world—Isaac Newton, Stephen Hawking, George Byron, Francis Bacon, John Keynes and more.

Speaking of Newton, someone solemnly told me in at least three different places in Cambridge, "This is the tree Newton was sitting under when he came up with his theory of gravity." Some also said they saw Hawking in his wheelchair at the market.

Cambridge was my first overseas studying experience. In the beginning, I had difficulties adjusting because of my limited knowledge of the English language and the University's methodology. There were times when I couldn't understand the professor, and it took hours to listen to the recorded lectures at home.

The bright light was that Dongwei continued to encourage and comfort me. "Slow down and change your attitude! You don't have to be among the first 5 percent of your class. You just need to graduate. Remember, that's your goal."

What a relief it was to find that exams didn't require a standard correct answer like they did in China. As long as one expressed one's views clearly, that was good enough. Therefore, my test results turned out quite good.

By the second semester, my language skills had improved, and I had adjusted well to Cambridge's educational methods and lifestyle. I was no longer so stressed out.

Of course, Dongwei at home was giving our daughter a lot of love and affection because I could not be there to hold her in my arms.

It wasn't easy to think of him as a father because he looks so youthful and innocent. But it's also no surprise that he really loves kids, and they love him in return. He can make friends with any child. Tiantian was completely in love with him. She was a little bit naughty around her grandparents or me, but whenever Daddy was around, she was very obedient.

Every day when her dad came home from work, Tiantian would open her arms and run to hug him. The minute he stepped in the door, she insisted that he pick her up. She couldn't speak yet, but she'd shout "En! En!" if he took too long. He couldn't even take off his jacket. Every evening at the sound of the doorbell, she would clap her hands and giggle, walking unsteadily toward the door.

Dongwei and I decided during my pregnancy that we would write everything down during Tiantian's growing-up years. For the nine months I would be in Cambridge, Dongwei would be both father and mother to our little one, and he would have to do the writing.

I like to read what Dongwei writes. His words are humorous and make me laugh. Here are a few of Dongwei's writings below, translated from Chinese.

Little Genius

Two or three months ago, Tiantian was first introduced to the computer and displayed enormous interest. She pounded on the keyboard very quickly and opened Microsoft Word twice without using the mouse.

I'm ashamed to admit that even to this day I have no idea how to open Microsoft Word without using the mouse. From the way she attacks the keyboard, I don't think it's the first time she's worked on a computer.

Later, she would often nudge me toward the computer, but I wouldn't oblige.

On January 1, a friend came to see us. She took a few pictures of Tiantian and emailed them to me. Yesterday, I downloaded the photos.

When little Tiantian realized the computer was on, she became very excited. She ran over to it and attacked it. She did it much faster and seemingly more knowledgeably than her mother.

I walked over to the television and put in a newly bought DVD for her. Then looking at the computer, I saw that she had opened Microsoft Excel, again without using the mouse.

She developed an interest in the blinking red light on the bottom of the mouse. As she played around with it, she would make a "Pa, pa" sound with her mouth. I have no idea whatsoever what she was trying to tell me.

With the DVD starting, I thought of switching off the computer. To my delight, the wallpaper had been changed to a photo of Tiantian and my friend.

Birth of 'Tiantian's' Name

Tiantian's uncle and my aunt chose this for her name at the same time, though they lived in different cities. When they found out her name was "Tianhui," they decided that her nickname should be Tiantian. Of course, they provided a long page of reasons for their decision.

In fact, Tiantian has a third name, chosen by my colleagues at work before she was born. One day a colleague asked, "Have you found a name for your baby? Here's a suggestion. If it's a girl, let's call her Xiao Hua (Little Flower). How does that sound?"

Therefore, whenever we talk about Tiantian at my office, my colleagues say, "How's that Little Flower at your house doing?"

Tiantian has liked little flowers very much ever since she was born. Maybe my colleagues hit on something intuitively. Whether it was small flowers embroidered on adult clothes, or those on the bed sheet, or even those on the sides of bowls, she would always stare at them very attentively. After she learned to crawl, she would always crawl to wherever she saw a flower.

We bought a bamboo mat for her to crawl on at home. There are three flowers embroidered on each of two corners of the mat. After she crawled to one corner and touched the three flowers, she turned around to look at the other three flowers on the other corner. I thought she was going to crawl to that corner.

But she was very lazy. She just rolled on the mat until she arrived at the other corner, and happily felt the three other flowers before giving me a toothless giggle.

In the midst of happiness, I also got a fright. She was only an inch away from the side of the bed.

So, a few days later, we placed a carpet on the floor so she could crawl on that. At least we wouldn't have to worry about her falling off the bed.

CHAPTER FIFTEEN

A few days after I arrived in Cambridge, I was shopping in the small downtown market when I suddenly saw a large banner hanging from a pole across a church in King's College. It said, "Falun Dafa is Good," in both Chinese and English.

The golden banner glistened in the afternoon sun. I stopped in my tracks and stared at it, for I hadn't seen anything like that in years. In mainland China, such images are normally followed by sirens and alarms and policemen arresting people. I could not help but walk over. A white-haired old lady smiled at me and handed me a flyer. She spoke with a thick southern Chinese accent. "Falun Dafa is good, Falun Gong is experiencing injustice," she said.

I was filled with a million feelings and words I wanted to say. Of course I knew that "Falun Dafa is good, Falun Gong is experiencing injustice"! I was utterly moved that there were people crying out loud in every corner of the world. Tears flowed down my face.

The old lady looked at me caringly. Her hand was still extended and she waited for me to take the flyer. I grabbed her arm and muttered softly, "I'm also a Falun Gong practitioner!" She immediately held my arms. Strangers we might be, but I immediately felt our hearts meet. A strong current swept through me, filling me with warm energy.

Like many other Falun Gong practitioners outside mainland China, practitioners in Cambridge were also doing all they could to expose the persecution of Falun Gong in China, and calling for an end to the persecution. Without any hesitation, they were spending their own money, time, and effort to help practitioners in mainland China—people they've never met.

It is such a group of people who have further strengthened my faith in Truthfulness, Compassion, and Tolerance.

———— • ————

Even though studies and research are treated solemnly in Cambridge, the scholastic atmosphere is active, and there are no restrictions on any thought. Many realms of so-called "superstition" in mainland China were areas of active research here. For example, I once went to a seminar that discussed how human thought influences matter.

Another thing that shocked me was that there was a lot of research about Marxism in Cambridge. A professor once told me that because Marxism originated in Europe, many European scholars feel obliged to study it properly. After being put into practice in over a dozen countries in the world, with similar overwhelmingly terrifying results, it is a theory that cannot be ignored.

The emergence of Marxism was bathed in idealism—the goal of creating a human utopia—and for this it has attracted countless avid followers. Yet in no country where it was actually put into practice did it end up doing what it claimed it would. Instead, poverty rose unchecked, compounded by corruption, environmental destruction, information blockages, dictatorships, and other communist phenomena.

The solemn attitude toward knowledge at Cambridge also extends into daily life. For example, a delicate, regular pattern is followed by most people, from eating and drinking to sports and other activities.

Speaking of food, the Formal Hall is unique in Cambridge, and the Formal Hall of each college has its own unique traits. Students and faculty members dress in black robes during dinner. Female visitors wear their most beautiful evening gowns, while male visitors wear tuxedoes. Tables are arranged beautifully, with flowers and candles. Knives and forks of all sizes are arranged by the sides of the plate, and you have to learn exactly how to work the order of these things.

There is also a complicated ritual spoken in Old English, which I couldn't understand at all. As for the quality of the food, that was secondary. As the Chinese saying goes, "We're eating culture."

Another important event in Cambridge is the May Ball. The tickets are extraordinarily expensive, the highest one being over 100 pounds, not to mention costs for clothing, jewelry and makeup. It's an exaggeratedly posh event, but young couples can enjoy spending a beautiful night together.

At the Ball, food, music, and performances begin in the evening, reach a climax around midnight, and continue until the next morning. Those who can survive till dawn are awarded the title of "survivor," and are photographed for the Survivor Picture at the break of dawn.

Without Dongwei by my side, I naturally had no motivation to go to such a ball. My classmates protested. "It would be such a pity if you left Cambridge without going to the May Ball! Just find a partner for the night, what does it matter? Your husband is so handsome, he's probably dancing with some other girl in Beijing right now."

I laughed at that. Having been married to Dongwei for so long, I knew him well. He's handsome, but his heart has always been pure and kind. After beginning cultivation, he became even more so. He would never engage in flirtatious behavior.

The feeling of separation was also a little different this time. All our phone calls and emails revolved around Tiantian. If a young couple were to hear our conversation, they would probably think it rather dull. "Does Tiantian like the new brand of milk?" "Did she have a good bowel movement today?"

But our feelings did not fade; instead, they evolved qualitatively. The child bears both our blood, and she unites our love into kinship. Dongwei is no longer just my love, but also my kin.

Life in England was beautiful and relaxed. The only trouble I had was that some of my friends often cautioned me, saying that many of the Chinese students here were also intelligence agents for the CCP. They warned me to be careful about what I said. It greatly tarnished the beauty of the Cambridge campus for me and its air of freedom.

It is because of intelligence agents that many Chinese students still do not dare to speak the truth even after leaving the direct control of the CCP.

I would often try to discuss the topic of Falun Gong with various Chinese students, but I found that every time I brought up the issue, they would change the subject. Even with some other slightly sensitive topics, they would not dare to discuss them. They continued to strictly "discipline" themselves as the CCP would want them to do.

To a certain extent, this kind of apathy and so-called neutrality allow the CCP's persecution of Falun Gong to be carried out and maintained so easily.

I planned to return to China after completing my studies, so I was always careful with those whom I thought might be spies for the CCP, and I decided not to contact other Falun Gong practitioners in Cambridge.

---·---

In March 2006, I was browsing the Internet in my room when I discovered that two witnesses who escaped from mainland China had exposed live organ harvesting atrocities by the CCP. They reported that China really does have a concentration camp that imprisons Falun Gong practitioners, and it uses them for live organ harvesting. After hearing this news, I remembered what the policewoman in the labor camp had told me about that concentration camp in the Northwest.

In disbelief, I quickly browsed through a few major mainland hospital websites and found advertisements for organ transplants. The advertisements claimed that they could obtain suitable donors within weeks.

This was just too suspicious! I was horror-stricken, and my first reaction was disbelief.

I stared into space for a long time, remembering how those Falun Gong practitioners who persisted against transformation had disappeared without a trace.

My heart slowly shattered, and my tears flowed like water gushing out of a broken riverbank. As I listened to the sound of rain outside my window, a line from ancient Chinese poet Bai Juyi's "Song of Eternal Sorrow" surfaced in my brain:

The night rain hears a grief-stricken sound from the bell.

A day later, a fellow Chinese student who had become a dear friend came to see me. He had a sharp mind, and his thought process was different from that of most people.

Earlier, when I had told him about the self-immolation incident in Tiananmen Square, he said, "I don't need to hear it from you guys [Falun Gong practitioners]. I know that the CCP's propaganda against Falun Gong is false, without a doubt. They say that

Falun Gong is superstitious, its practitioners commit suicide, self-immolate, refuse to take drugs, that Falun Gong has the support of overseas political anti-Chinese forces and has political goals. These allegations are contradictory. Think about it, how can a suicidal, self-immolating, superstitious group of individuals have political goals, and be supported by overseas anti-Chinese forces?"

Now when I told him about the live organ harvesting, he said solemnly, "It is not easy to ascertain whether this is true or not, but one thing is clear. If this is fake, then it must have been arranged by the CCP."

I was taken aback. "Why would they do that?"

He responded, "Think about it! If it's fake, it'll be easy enough to find out. By then, though, Falun Gong practitioners would have broadcast this thing worldwide. Wouldn't it be humiliating to practitioners if the CCP could prove them wrong? Isn't that exactly what the CCP would like to achieve? If it wasn't true, the CCP would immediately broadcast this information, and invite officials from abroad to come to China and see for themselves. All you need to do is wait and see if the CCP blocks this information on the web, like it did with the Tiananmen Massacre and the self-immolation incident. If they decide to filter this out, that would mean it must be true."

He paused. "If it's true, then it's too hideous. But thinking about it, some Jews escaped from the Nazi concentration camps during the Second World War. At the time, most people didn't believe them, and that delayed rescue efforts. Only after the Allied troops captured many of the labor camps were the atrocities and crimes against humanity exposed. And only then did the world vow, 'Never Again.'"

———◦———

Spring break came during the Easter holidays, a popular time to take a vacation in England. But my heart was heavy, and I didn't feel like taking a vacation.

Then came another blow. A friend from the political and judicial circles in mainland China told me that the CCP had launched another round of persecution against Falun Gong. What made it even worse for me was the news that they were targeting "young and highly educated" people, especially those who had returned to mainland China after studying overseas.

He advised me to remain abroad for a while.

A few days later, I discovered on the Internet a confidential document from a 610 Office[19] in Hebei Province that confirmed what I had been told. The document called for a full investigation of all Falun Gong practitioners, saying that units should "register every person" and focus on the "Three Highs, Three Longs, and Three Outs."

The Three Highs, I recall, referred to "High education, High IQ, and Highly skilled in one's profession." I don't remember what the Three Longs and Three Outs were. The document also said, "This is a secret mission. Perform your duty and keep this effort under wraps. It must be kept confidential under all circumstances." It also stated, "We cannot let the international community discover this information and chastise us."

There are many people from my generation, including many of my classmates, who had studied overseas. Over 90 percent of Dongwei's former biology classmates had studied overseas. We also had the opportunity to do so, but chose to remain in China. It was our home, after all. I have always had a deep love for my homeland.

Their target would definitely include Dongwei and me. Would I really face danger if I returned? What had happened to my homeland? Couldn't they leave us in peace?

Although I had knowledge of these horrible things happening, I still could not grasp the extent of it. I held in my heart the thought that I might be lucky. Dongwei was so busy at work, and he had to take care of our baby. Every day, he went straight home from work. What reason could they find to arrest him? We hadn't written any more appeal letters.

I called Dongwei and asked him to be careful. He only told me that his workplace was holding an international conference on rule of law, and that he was extremely busy.

He also proudly told me that our daughter was becoming more and more like him. "She's showing more and more signs of being left-handed. She seems to use her left hand whenever she does anything."

---

19 610 Office—the name of an extra-legal task force established June 10, 1999 (hence the name), by Jiang Zemin, to lead the persecution against Falun Gong. It has a network of branches throughout China down to the level of neighborhoods and is granted a broad range of authority for fulfilling its task.

CHAPTER SIXTEEN

May 19, 2006, was a Friday. I was finishing my thesis. During that time, I spent more than ten hours a day working at the computer.

Chinese students at Cambridge University would get together for a party every weekend to share some good home-cooked food and provide a bit of escape from the intensity of student life.

That Friday, the party was at the apartment of one of our class-mates. After dinner we strolled back to our rooms, enjoying the sweet, fragrant scent of spring flowers.

The Cambridge grounds are covered with fresh grass and beauti-ful flowers during the month of May. The students in Cambridge looked so happy and lovely.

After I arrived at my room, I called my husband, as I always did. The time difference between Cambridge and Beijing is eight hours. Since it was the weekend and I could sleep in late, it wasn't a problem for me to stay up late talking to him. It was Saturday morning in Beijing, but since there was a toddler at home my husband would almost certainly be awake.

Usually on Saturdays, Dongwei would take Tiantian to the nearby Purple Bamboo Park for a walk after we talked on the phone.

The phone on the other end rang and rang, much longer than usual. Finally I heard my father pick up.

"Hello?" His voice was hoarse.

"What are you doing?" I asked. "How come you took so long to pick up?"

When my father heard my voice, he hesitated. "Oh! Let me tell you something. But don't panic. Dongwei was arrested!"

My head started swimming. I couldn't say a word. All I could do was listen to my father describing what had happened that night.

He and my mother were taking care of Tiantian, who was now 16 months old. When Dongwei came home from work, little Tiantian rushed up to him as usual. Her daddy picked her up and gave her hugs and kisses.

Less than five minutes later, Dongwei heard someone knocking at the door.

He didn't think anything and opened the door. Seven or eight policemen burst into the room.

I felt as if a gigantic stone was pressing on my heart, and I couldn't breathe. My heart could hardly endure the pain.

The police ordered my husband to provide everything immediately, otherwise they would ransack our home. Dongwei told them he didn't know what they were talking about.

The police answered that they were looking for copies of the *Nine Commentaries on the Communist Party*. They said that someone had reported him to the police.

Dongwei said he didn't have any copies of the book, so the policemen began searching the house. They ransacked our bedroom with its sweet wedding photos, the neat study room, and even the baby's room. They turned everything upside down.

After searching our house, they confiscated several Falun Gong books but didn't find any copies of the *Nine Commentaries*.

They arrested him anyway. They also confiscated our computers, so we lost all our recent photos—all of Dongwei's photography, and many of our beautiful memories.

My elderly parents watched as the police arrested their son-in-law. Then they were left to comfort their granddaughter and clean up the mess.

And my baby had to see all this.

Whenever I think of it, tears come to my eyes.

———◆———

After Dongwei's second arrest, my life became a nightmare. My heart felt as if it was pressed down by a monstrous rock, and I experienced periods when I was unable to move, unable to breathe. I felt as if something was pounding in my stomach. The physical pain was excruciating, and it enveloped my entire being. I could neither eat nor drink. I had to force myself to eat.

Yet I knew that I could not have a nervous breakdown. I had to rescue him, and at the same time I had to complete my studies. I did my research during the day in the library and wrote my thesis at night. I made phone calls to everyone I could think of in mainland China to ask for help. I only slept two or three hours a night. If not for the Falun Gong exercises, I would not have been able to keep up such a demanding schedule.

Initially, I thought to resolve this issue through legal means in China. I thought, "It's Beijing after all, and it will hold the 2008 Olympics, so how can they just arrest someone without due cause? The whole affair is just too absurd!"

Every time I made calls to mainland China, I suffered rude and unreasonable admonishment by the police, or coldness from those I asked for help.

I felt hopelessness enveloping me, and several times a day I would escape to hidden places and weep.

I called the Haidian Public Security Bureau several times and told them of their illegal actions. One told me he couldn't provide any information to overseas callers. Another said, "If you think what we're doing is illegal, why don't you sue us?" Another said, "He was arrested by the Internal Security Team. We're only detaining him. You should contact them."

The staff from the Internal Security Team hung up the phone the minute they heard the word Falun Gong. When I called again, the man claimed it was a private number. I said, "I just called and you told me you're the Internal Security Team." Then he started swearing and threatened to throw me in prison.

I wrote letters to their superiors, the Beijing Municipal Government, but I never received a response.

In late June, a friend of mine from mainland China told me that Dongwei had been sentenced to two and a half years of re-education through labor. I felt as if I had been struck by lightning.

Perhaps I wouldn't have been so upset if I didn't know what the labor camps were like. Having already suffered that torture and degradation, I feared for his safety and sanity!

I decided to file an appeal.

Our aged parents tried to visit him several times, but staff from the Haidian Detention Center denied them visiting rights.

Later, I begged a classmate from law school to be Dongwei's defense lawyer on our appeal.

Under existing Chinese law, it does not matter what crime one has committed, a lawyer has the right to meet the defendant. However, when my lawyer went to Haidian Detention Center to meet with Dongwei, he was told that Falun Gong practitioners are prohibited from seeing their lawyers.

Even murderers are allowed to see their lawyers.

Later, this lawyer friend of mine gave up, saying there's no way to defend a Falun Gong practitioner.

Three months after Dongwei's arrest, our parents officially received the so-called "Sentence to Re-education Through Labor" verdict from the Judicial Section of the Haidian Public Security Bureau. The message said that Dongwei had been sentenced to two and half years of re-education through labor for "hiding 80 copies of Falun Gong propaganda materials" at home.

My tears had already run dry. I can't express the pain and distress I suffered. I know there are no laws that say one cannot have Falun Gong-related materials at home. And I also know we never even had these 80 so-called propaganda materials at home. The police leveled false accusations so that Dongwei would be sentenced to prison.

———•———

It is now January 2008. The wound seems to have recovered on the surface now, but with Dongwei still imprisoned, the pain has not abated. I feel excruciating pain whenever I think about his suffering. The thought of him being tortured in the labor camp is unbearable.

Throughout the week before Dongwei's arrest, Tiantian would wake up in the middle of the night crying and refuse to calm down. Dongwei was worried that she wasn't feeling well. Maybe she sensed something coming.

The people who came to take my husband away wore police uniforms and claimed that they were from the Beijing Police Bureau, Haidian branch. But they didn't leave any written evidence or paperwork. They also did not have a warrant. He was simply abducted.

It has been almost two years since Dongwei was arrested, almost two years since I last talked to him. This is by far the longest time we've been apart since we met 20 years ago. The last time something like this happened, both of us were imprisoned in labor camps.

Now he is imprisoned again in the notorious Beijing Tuanhe Labor Camp, the same one he was kept in before. Meanwhile, our daughter has been without her parents for 20 months. She will turn 3 this month.

Whenever I read Dongwei's blog on the web about Tiantian, and think of the suffering and torture he faces in the labor camp, I can't stop crying.

Especially when reading the last article he wrote on his blog, I feel deep sadness. The date on the blog is May 15, 2006, four days before his arrest, suspended as if frozen in time.

Water Knows the Answer

Last year I read a book review online about the book *Water Knows the Answer*. The author discovered through a series of experiments with water crystals that water retains a lot of information.

I was astounded reading about some of the extraordinary research methods and conclusions. When different languages were used to say "thank you" to water, the water molecules crystallized into very pretty hexagonal shapes. When you say, "hate" however, the water doesn't crystallize or will crystallize into ugly shapes. Listening to classical music, the water creates very beautiful crystals, while heavy rock or techno music stops the crystallization of water entirely. The entire book is filled with hundreds of colorful pictures of water crystals.

This discovery imparts at least two meanings. The first is philosophical. Modern science believes in matter over mind. That is, the mind is subordinate to the material world. Yet these experiments give us the opportunity to reconsider the nature of the mind. Mind and matter are actually one.

Stephen Hawking wrote in his book *A Brief History of Time*, "Any physical theory is always provisional, in the sense that it is only a hypothesis: you can never prove it. No matter how many times the results of experiments agree with some theory, you can never be sure that the next time the result will not contradict the theory. On the other hand, you can disprove a theory by finding even a single observation that disagrees with the predictions of the theory."[20]

In fact, philosophical theories' predictions often speak truth. The only problem is that philosophy is not a subject most people find interesting. They are just busy earning money, and do not have time to ponder philosophical questions.

The other meaning is practical. Just as it states on the book's cover page, "Why does the world need praise?" If even a drop of water can feel the difference between good and bad, a child must definitely know, even if he or she does not know how to express or communicate it.

Tiantian eats, drinks, sleeps, and even showers amidst our praise. "Good girl! Pretty girl! Little Beauty!" are some of the things we tell her. Sometimes, when I hear these words, I am reminded of resumes I've seen.[21]

My mother tells me that when she asks Tiantian, "Do you miss your daddy?" most of the time she will say "No."

But when she plays games, she often calls, "Daddy, where are you? How are you doing? I miss you so much."

Tiantian was such a happy child when Dongwei was around. But after her father was abducted, her emotions have become unstable. She often throws tantrums, and she wakes up crying in the middle of the night.

I called home one day and heard her grandmother say to her, "Tell your mom that you've been eating and sleeping well."

She immediately said, "Mom, I can't eat or sleep well."

Grandma rushed to say, "Don't say that, your mother will be worried! Tell her you've been a good girl and have been very obedient."

"Mom, I've been a good girl and obedient."

I asked, "Can you do that?"

"No, I can't."

Dongwei and I are both missing this time with our child. Longing and missing have replaced the blissful, happy feeling of being a parent.

Her grandmother recorded some of Tiantian's funny incidents in a journal, and Tiantian loves to hear her own stories. Before she turned 3, she would often ask Grandma or Grandpa, "Can we study

---

20 Steven Hawking, *A Brief History of Time*. (New York: Bantam, 1998), 10

21 In China, many women write words such as beautiful, kind, and pretty on their resumes, hoping to increase their chances of being hired.

Tiantian's funny incidents from when she was younger?" It was as if she was already grown up.

When I call her, the most difficult question she asks me is, "Where's Daddy?" I don't know how to answer her, and I often try to change the subject.

"Do you miss Mommy?"

"Yes, I miss Mommy, but I miss Daddy even more."

Sometimes I cannot imagine that I am talking to a 2-year-old. I reply hurriedly, "Don't be anxious. Daddy will be back soon."

"How soon is soon?" she asks.

Her heartbreaking question reminds me of one I used to ask my parents: "How long is eternity?"

———•———

Mothers often like to talk about their children, but whenever the conversation turns to children, I can't face it and will try to run away. It's true that children are the most beloved topic for mothers, but I never have much to say.

Sometimes people say, "You're a very strong person. You don't seem to miss your daughter."

I only reply with a smile. But a line in Rabindranath Tagore's "The Farthest Distance" crosses through my mind:

I have to pretend that I don't care about you at all,
    While I can't help missing you.

Alas, my little daughter, I can't help missing you with every fiber of my being.

With Dongwei imprisoned in a labor camp, and me forced to remain overseas, our young daughter is left with our aging parents. Our harmonious family has been torn apart.

Nevertheless, I believe it shall not last long, for heavenly laws will right wrongs and the world will become balanced again.

———•———

During the World Cup soccer season in Cambridge, discussions on campus were quite heated in the evenings. Young students would gather on the field to watch the competition, just like my family and I used to sit on a field to watch movies when I was young. If the England team won, students sometimes celebrated with fireworks.

The joyous mood was in stark contrast to my situation.

Sometimes, after forcing myself to eat something, I would also go to the field and sit among the students, hoping to be affected by the joyous atmosphere. However, more often than not, I would sit with tears running down my face among the happy crowd, thinking about Dongwei.

The weather in England is unpredictable. It rains without warning, and most people there are unconcerned by the rain. Seeing pedestrians walking in the rain is also great to watch. Normally, when I encountered a storm, I would hide in a café and drink a cup of coffee. Seeing the English people walking in the rain through the window, I would often smile. They were so courageous in the rain. They didn't care if it was pouring rain or thundering, they simply kept walking without a frown.

After Dongwei's arrest, I no longer hid from the rain. I walked in the rain, just like the English. I let the rain wash away my tears. My tears tasted bitter when they arrived at my mouth. I thought they should taste salty, and I wondered if their bitterness had to do with the chilling storm or the bitterness in my heart.

Sometimes I cannot imagine how people like me and Dongwei could ever be persecuted. How can anyone else guarantee that they will not become a target one day? Even though many people are beneficiaries of various economic interests, they are still in danger because China's current society is unfair and unjust. Didn't we used to be respected members of society, "the foundation of our nation"? That didn't make a difference when the time came to persecute us.

Dongwei is in my mind at all times. I wish to see him, even in my dreams. However, because I sleep so little, when I finally fall asleep, I do not dream.

The farthest distance in the world
Is not when I stand in front of you, yet you can't see my love,
But when we know without a doubt of each other's love
Yet we cannot be together.

—Rabindranath Tagore

CHAPTER SEVENTEEN

M y heart was heavy. After nine months of strenuous studying and finally graduating from Cambridge University, I could not return to China. I could not reunite with my little girl and be with my family as my heart had planned.

In the months after Dongwei's arrest, I tried many approaches to have him released—formal, informal, legal, illegal. I was not successful.

Every time I called mainland China, I would break into tears after getting off the phone. The disregard for the law, the irrational attitude, the apathy toward others' suffering, and the taking of pleasure in others' misfortunes formed an agonizing mixture of hopelessness and anger inside me.

I finally realized that my actions were just like the sheep asking the wolf that abducted it to consider how nice the sheep is, and begging the wolf to be kind and not eat the sheep.

This realization finally did the trick. I could discard any fantasy I still harbored about the CCP. After all the suffering I'd experienced, I had let go of most of the ideas I had been nurturing about the CCP. But I still clung to wishful thinking about Chinese government workers who were part of the CCP's system. After all, I used to be one of them, and I was still in contact with these people.

I knew that many of them had a kind heart and a side that wanted to do good. Many of them had even desired to be instrumental in reforming the Party. In my naïveté I still thought the government employees I knew were my good friends and classmates. In my mind I reasoned, "How could they not help me? Besides, we've done nothing wrong."

Now I finally understood. Even people who still held decent and moral thoughts could not speak for themselves in a world run by the CCP. Even if these people could differentiate between right and wrong, they were bound by invisible ties and could not make right decisions.

Even the former CCP General Secretaries Hu Yaobang and Zhao Ziyang could not change the CCP from within. What could ordinary workers do, even if they had the will to do good? And many decent people were dragged into the quagmire created by the CCP and really had become morally corrupt.

———◆———

Faith is something that develops from within and forms the spirituality of the individual. Faith is the world where one's spirit resides. It holds one's inner thoughts toward God and others, toward life and the universe.

It is beyond what a political party can or should control.

Could the CCP really be filled with so much hatred toward those with faith simply because of the desire to stay in power?

I realized after reading the *Nine Commentaries on the Communist Party* that the CCP is not simply a political party, it is a specter that possesses people, holding them in its clutches.

I can see it clearly now. When one encourages some people to quit the Party, their reactions are often abnormally passionate. The specter of the communist regime is at work.

A friend of mine tried to encourage her husband to withdraw from the Party. Her husband actually did not think highly of the CCP. Yet he went into a temper tantrum and nearly threw her off the bed. When she asked him afterward why he had flared up, he could not explain it.

A friend of Dongwei's, who used to call me sister-in-law out of respect, threw a fit and began swearing at me when I tried to encourage him to quit the CCP.

If people really think about it, they will realize that this abnormal behavior is a wake-up call. Only by discarding the CCP's influence can one's true nature be revealed.

How fortunate, then, that over 30 million Chinese people have now formally quit the CCP and its related youth organizations.[22]

The first time Dongwei and I were arrested, almost everyone around us was really angry that it had happened. They found it unthinkable that such good people were sentenced to a prison term. But after Dongwei was arrested again, even though most of our friends still wanted to help, I had to listen to some unreasonable remarks.

Someone told me, "I no longer believe what you said about retribution and good rewards. Dongwei is such a good person, isn't he? Why does he have to suffer retribution? He's in a labor camp again. The way I see it, good people suffer retribution for being good!"

Dongwei's parents even felt ashamed that their son was imprisoned in a labor camp again, and they didn't dare tell anyone. I told my 80-year-old father-in-law on the phone, "Your son is in a labor camp because he is living by Truthfulness, Compassion, and Tolerance. The dishonorable ones are those who arrest good people!"

Though Dongwei's father has always adored me, he flared up. "If you think *Zhen-Shan-Ren* is so good, then wait until I die before living by those principles! Can't you give me two years of peace while I'm still breathing?"

Since his son was arrested, Dongwei's elderly father has become deaf and can only hear with a hearing aid. And now he can see out of only one of his eyes, which we all feel is due to sadness. Succumbing to the CCP hasn't brought him any benefit.

It finally dawned on me that this persecution of good people not only destroyed my family, but was also destroying the moral fiber and feelings of many people and contributing to the downfall of humanity.

If people don't believe in retribution for evil and reward for doing good, how can they be stopped from doing evil? Is there anything they will dare not do?

This situation is perilous for all humankind. Though it is more obvious under the CCP, it is evident in other countries as well.

After realizing all this, I cannot allow good and compassionate people to be persecuted by the evil. I must do all I can to rescue Dongwei and let the world know what is happening. We have to help restore people's belief in being good and righteous.

---

22 As of June 2013, over 140 million people have quit the Party. This number also includes members of the communist youth organizations and retirees who have renounced their association with the Party.

In July, Cambridge University's Jesus College held a get-together. Even though it promised to be a great event, I was in no mood to go. But I'd already promised a friend, so I forced myself.

I did not realize it, but several English government officials would be present. Apparently, though most English prime ministers studied at Oxford, a great number of ministers and other officials are alumni of Cambridge. Many visited Cambridge frequently.

During introductions I learned that one was an official at the U.K. Foreign and Commonwealth Office. I thought perhaps I could ask him to help in my rescue efforts for Dongwei. But how should I approach him? Would he think that arrested people must be bad and refuse to help me?

To my surprise, this official started walking in my direction. As he passed by, I summoned all the strength I had to call his name. Although my words weren't clear, he heard me and stopped, looking at me with concern.

"I need your help," I said.

"My pleasure," he grinned.

I got straight to the point. "My husband has been arrested in Beijing!"

He was shocked. "Why?"

"Because of Falun Gong!"

Hearing the words Falun Gong, he nodded. I wanted to explain further, but he patted my shoulder comfortingly. "I understand completely, you don't have to elaborate." From his expression, I could tell that he was fully aware of the persecution.

That day, my SOS tour to save Dongwei began. I told his story everywhere I went, asking for the help of all compassionate people.

———•———

Nine months after I arrived, I graduated from Cambridge. That morning, the town was as tranquil and beautiful as ever. When I got on the bus, I knew that this would be the most beautiful place I'd ever live.

I traveled to San Francisco, where the headquarters of Dongwei's company was located. In San Francisco, I met with the heads of the Asia Foundation and asked for help.

I got involved in press conferences and initiated news releases. I made the most of all the media available to me and asked for their help and support. I asked people in Chinatown and all through

San Francisco to sign my petition. I called upon the international society for help.

I don't remember how many places I visited after I graduated from Cambridge, how many letters I sent, or how many government officials or government representatives I talked to.

Their sympathy and concern strengthened my belief that it is not a disgrace for Dongwei to be imprisoned for his belief in Truthfulness, Compassion, and Tolerance.

In an August 29, 2006, Amnesty International press release, Dongwei was named a prisoner of conscience, and the message was to the entire world: "Help rescue Falun Gong practitioners in Chinese prisons."

On September 7, the European Parliament passed a resolution that included a clause calling for Dongwei's release. The United Nations also listed Dongwei among one of the most urgent cases. The German and Swiss ministries of foreign affairs also sent letters in support of my cause. Many other governmental officials and non-governmental organizations from different countries wrote to express their support and help.

I walked through three buildings where the American Congress is housed and talked to many officials. In August 2007, some U.S. Congress members wrote letters demanding Dongwei's release.

In California, where I currently reside, some cities passed resolutions to condemn the persecution and demand Dongwei's release. Many other cities are in the process of passing similar resolutions.

Throughout the SOS tour, I often cried, but it was no longer out of pain and hopelessness, but because my heart was deeply touched by all the support I found, and also out of gratitude. I am often told, "Your husband is a lucky guy."

They must mean to encourage me to be a strong and brave wife. I often reply, "Yes, he is very lucky." Not because of me, but because he has received the support of so many people who have never met him. All these people have lightened my burden and showed me humanity, which illuminates my darkness.

As long as my husband is imprisoned, I will not forsake my quest to rescue him. I will tell everyone I know and meet about Dongwei's story until he can walk out with his head held high.

I know there are also many, many people who have suffered similar injustice. In my effort to rescue Dongwei, I also need to raise awareness and help stop this persecution as soon as possible.

I want to share a piece of truth that is carved into my heart and written in the *Nine Commentaries*:

> *Even though the CCP appears to possess all the resources and violent apparatus in the country, if every citizen believes in the power of the truth and safeguards morality, the evil specter of the CCP will lose the foundation for its existence. All resources may instantly return to the hands of the just. That is when the rebirth of China will take place.*[23]

———•———

Years ago, I saw many of our friends and classmates emigrate from China. Yet not once did I wish to follow in their footsteps. It would have never occurred to me that someone as emotionally dependent as I might someday live alone overseas.

Sometimes I have thought that if not for my refusing to emigrate from China, Dongwei and I might have come to the United States a long time ago, and he would have escaped arrest. Whenever that thought enters my mind, I feel deep regret, and I wish I could change the past.

The two years since I last saw him have been the loneliest of my life. I have no idea what he is facing, or how he is doing.

I have written many letters to him, but I have no idea if he has received them. The labor camps often refuse to give letters to Falun Gong practitioners. Even though he used to tease me because my handwriting is not as pretty as his, I'm sure a wife's words would strengthen his resolve and warm his heart.

I remember a verse in an ancient Chinese poem:

> *Alone in a faraway land,*
> *missing my family doubles every holiday season.*

My heart grows especially heavy during Christmas and other holidays, when the streets are filled with happy people. It is difficult to see the malls packed, with everyone choosing a gift for their beloved.

Standing among the crowd, I can only think, "What would I buy for him if he were not in a labor camp?" Maybe I would choose a pair of gloves to warm his hands, and tea to warm his heart during

---

23 The Epoch Times, *Nine Commentaries on the Communist Party*. (Mountain View, Calif: Broad Press, 2005), last page

the wintertime. Or perhaps a golden tie, for he has never worn such a color. I imagine how he would look wearing this tie.

———•———

Last year, during the Chinese New Year, I called my parents, but no one answered. I tried a little while later and still no one answered. I kept calling all day, but no one picked up.

I could no longer bear it and decided to call Dongwei's parents. My mother-in-law told me that Tiantian was very sick and had been hospitalized. Dongwei's sister had rushed to the hospital, and said that I should call her cell phone.

Dongwei's sister answered her cell, and I learned that my Tiantian had been sick for several days and was unable to eat. She had a high fever and would vomit anything she ate. She was hospitalized immediately. All the hospital rooms were full, so her bed was in the hallway. She had been receiving infusions for three days.

My sister-in-law told me she heard other sick children asking for their mothers to hold them. Then they'd fall asleep peacefully in their mothers' arms. Only my daughter was saying, "Grandma, hold me!" My elderly mother held her for the entire night, unable to sleep.

After I hung up, I was filled with sorrow. I was without my husband, child, parents, or any family. I was alone and unable to be there for them when they needed me.

I took out a picture of Tiantian. She was so cute, but I could see the sadness in her eyes. There was no carefree smile that should have been on a 2-year-old's face. I was heartbroken, and I wanted to cry uncontrollably.

Just as I was about to break out in tears, the doorbell rang, and I got up and answered. It was an older practitioner who had come by to pick something up. She did not leave right away, and we chatted for a while. Before she left, she told me, "Do take good care of yourself."

After closing the door, I decided not to cry. I thought that the heavens were hoping I would become strong. Heaven does not want me to drown in sorrow.

I sat there and remembered all the hardships I had suffered over the past few years. Slowly and gradually, a strong feeling arose in my heart. I was filled with a strength I had never felt before, and my heart was filled with peace and tranquility.

I am absolutely sure that no matter how hard the path before me might be, as long as I follow the principles of Truthfulness, Compassion, and Tolerance, I will never fall. I shall forever stand strong between heaven and earth.

January 2008
Los Angeles, California

Tiantian

EPILOGUE

On July 19, 2008, I was in Washington, D.C., participating in activities appealing for an end to the persecution of Falun Gong. It was the eve of the ninth anniversary of the onset of the persecution.

I received a long-distance phone call from Dongwei's sister. She told me that Dongwei might be released the next day and that she would go to the labor camp to pick him up first thing in the morning. Even though I had always been confident this day would arrive, still I was overcome with joy. And Dongwei would finally get to see our daughter—they hadn't seen each other in over two years.

On July 20, I got up early at 5 a.m. It was 5 p.m. in Beijing. I decided this was a good time to call. The phone rang for a long time and no one picked up. I called five minutes later. No one picked up. Ten minutes later, no one. I didn't think they'd be in the mood to go out the first day Dongwei was back, so where could they be? After 20 minutes, still no one. My uneasiness grew into anxiety. Two hours passed and still no answer.

I decided that I must still participate in the day's activities on Capitol Hill. Just when I was about to leave home, I decided to try one last time. My sister-in-law answered.

"Where did you guys go?" I asked.

"Nowhere. We just got back."

"Didn't you go to get him first thing in the morning?"

"Yeah. We were taken directly in a police car to the police station for questioning. We just got back."

Then I remembered. That was exactly what had happened before.

Dongwei took the phone. "It's me."

I didn't know what to say. "Are you okay?"

"Yeah, I'm still doing all right. Just a little tired."

I knew he was making light of his situation, but I didn't press the issue.

We chatted briefly, then I told him, "I need to go to an activity." I didn't say what activity, but Dongwei knew what I meant. July 20 is too familiar to every Falun Gong practitioner around the world. He said, "Yes, definitely, go ahead."

Thousands of Falun Gong practitioners gather on Capitol Hill every year on July 20, calling for an end to the persecution. Just thinking about the countless practitioners who are currently imprisoned is enough motivation for me to press on.

Of course, for me, I wanted Dongwei and our daughter to come to the United States as soon as possible, where we could reunite as a family.

In the process of speaking with the U.S. Citizenship and Immigration Services and the State Department, things went unbelievably smoothly. A few months later, Dongwei and 4-year-old Tiantian arrived at the Los Angeles airport.

Dongwei had much more white hair than I remembered, but he was still the same person that I knew. Our daughter, however, had become a complete stranger. I was so relieved when I took her in my arms, and she hugged me and said "Mama," very naturally. It was like she had gone out for a few days to play and had just returned home. I was filled with gratitude—it must be God protecting the good, helping us reach a good solution at the end of this tribulation.

My wish is for everyone to understand the truth behind the persecution of Falun Gong, to become good in their hearts and be protected by God, so that we can all move through the present turbulence and have a great future.

November 2011

DONGWEI'S EPILOGUE

I often imagined myself flying out of the Beijing Capital Airport to the United States. Many times I would be working in the slave labor camp, or standing on the court under the scorching sun where Falun Gong practitioners were forced to stand for prolonged periods—which the labor camp called "formation training," though the intention was to punish—and I imagined my daughter would be holding my hand and asking me, "How long before we see Mom?"

After being released from the labor camp, I felt that I had simply been transferred from a small prison into a larger one—Chinese society. Even though I had spoken with my wife several times over the phone after I got home, we both knew our phone was tapped, so she didn't dare say anything about what was going on outside.

I vividly remember getting off the plane at the Los Angeles Airport, holding my daughter's hand and searching the crowd anxiously for my wife. Finally I spotted her.

She made her usual gesture, as if I had just come home from a business trip, though this was by far the longest separation we'd endured in 20 years.

Hongwei gently picked up Tiantian, who didn't seem uncomfortable with her mother at all, despite the years that separated them.

It was only after I arrived in the United States that my wife began to tell me about the rescuing activities she had initiated outside of China. I was deeply touched that so many people, whom I've never had the honor of meeting, have worked so hard to help me. The way I see it, only by continuing to live a life according to the principles of Truthfulness, Compassion, and Tolerance can I express my gratitude and live up to their expectations.

I also learned the answers to many questions that had bothered me when I was in China. For example, after being released, I went back home to see my elderly parents. The local police immediately came to my parents' home, saying that they had received a call from Beijing Public Security. They threatened me, telling me not to accept any interviews by foreign journalists. I was puzzled—how would foreign journalists know me?

It turned out that Falun Gong practitioners outside China, and also Amnesty International, had been calling for my release for over two years.

On a wall in the main hall of the labor camp, there is a huge poster with a list of our "rights," including freedom of communication. An elderly policeman spoke the truth about it. "Rights? That's just for outside people to see."

Every piece of mail that goes in or out of the labor camp is carefully read and inspected by police. After arriving in the United States, I realized the labor camp had received many letters addressed to me, and of course almost all the letters from outside mainland China had been confiscated.

Amnesty International once held a write-a-thon campaign to call for my release, but I never received any of those letters.

----•----

One weekend, my family stepped out of a beautiful Los Angeles theater after watching Shen Yun Performing Arts. I sat on a bench with images of the wonderful dances and costumes still floating in my head, savoring the beautiful 5,000 years of Chinese culture. I wondered to myself why I'd never seen a lovely performance like Shen Yun in China.

It was a warm, clear day. The sun shone brightly, illuminating seagulls cruising through the air. Looking at the snow-capped mountains in the distance, breathing the air of freedom that I now enjoy, everything that happened as recently as two years ago felt like it was in a previous life.

I can't tell you how much I wish that the same feeling of freedom was found not only in the United States, but that all the people in China were able to live their lives in freedom, with dignity and honor.

That day, I believe, is not far away.

November 2011

AFTERWORD

When my husband began practicing Falun Dafa in 2009, I remember thinking that a story about a Chinese practitioner could be quite interesting. What was it like growing up in the mysterious land of China? How had the persecution affected this person?

When I began practicing Falun Dafa a year later, my diabetes began to get better, and soon I was able to work for the first time in over a decade. I was delighted—I had my life back! Now that I was feeling well almost all the time, I began to ask around to see if anyone had a story they were willing to share. Someone put me in touch with Hongwei Lou.

As I was reading her story, I knew right away that it was the one I was looking for. I thought the story itself was enthralling, yet the English needed smoothing, and I decided it should be arranged chronologically in the usual style of autobiographies. The book needed me. I untangled many time threads and asked Ms. Lou to write about her childhood and elaborate on some other things. She graciously agreed to work with me despite her busy schedule. She answered many questions when I didn't understand something and proofread the final copy for accuracy.

I've been truly moved by her story. One evening when I was home going over the manuscript once again, my husband was sitting at his desk nearby, and I told him: "Just ignore the sobbing. Occupational hazard."

Throughout my handling of the manuscript and subsequent notes from Ms. Lou, I tried to use a light touch and not change the meaning of her words, and to retain as much of the flavor as possible.

The girl on the front cover is Tiantian at age 7.

Recently, Dongwei's current employer got word of the book and was eager to write something about him, calling him his "most valuable employee":

> *"Dongwei is extremely hardworking and very responsible. He jumps in to help in many areas, even if they fall outside his assignments and he may not get credit for them. He always likes to help others.*
>
> *"He is so dedicated in his work that it inspires others to work harder as well. We feel he is a model employee and are so glad he joined our company, which as a result had record revenues last year in several lines of business."*

Here is a video of Dongwei made by Amnesty International:
http://vimeo.com/16943242
or http://www.amnestyusa.org/news/multimedia/
your-letters-made-a-difference-in-my-life

Kathryn Lovett
kathryn@remembertruth.info
May 2013

A portion of the proceeds from the sale of this book will be donated to Friends of Falun Gong, a nonprofit that supports freedom of belief for those who practice Falun Gong.